Pocket Guide to APA Style

FOURTH EDITION

Pocket Guide to APA Style

FOURTH EDITION

Robert Perrin
Indiana State University

WADSWORTH
CENGAGE Learning·

Australia • Brazil • Japan • Korea • Mexico • Singapore • Spain •
United Kingdom • United States

WADSWORTH
CENGAGE Learning

Pocket Guide to APA Style: Fourth Edition
Robert Perrin

Senior Publisher: Lyn Uhl

Acquiring Sponsoring Editor: Kate Derrick

Development Editor: Kelli Strieby

Editorial Assistant: Elizabeth Reny

Media Editor: Janine Tangney

Marketing Manager: Stacey Purviance

Marketing Coordinator: Ryan Ahern

Content Project Manager: Aimee Chevrette Bear

Art Director: Jill Ort

Print Buyer: Betsy Donaghey

Rights Acquisition Specialist: Katie Huha

Production Service: MPS Limited, a Macmillan Company

Cover Designer: Anne Dauchy, Hecht Design

Compositor: MPS Limited, a Macmillan Company

Library of Congress Control Number: 2010930337

ISBN-13: 978-0-495-91263-7
ISBN-10: 0-495-91263-8

Wadsworth
20 Channel Center Street
Boston, MA 02210
USA

Cengage Learning is a leading provider of customized learning solutions with office locations around the globe, including Singapore, the United Kingdom, Australia, Mexico, Brazil and Japan. Locate your local office at **international.cengage.com/region**

Cengage Learning products are represented in Canada by Nelson Education, Ltd.

For your course and learning solutions, visit **www.cengage.com.**
Purchase any of our products at your local college store or at our preferred online store **www.cengagebrain.com.**

Printed in the United States of America
1 2 3 4 5 6 7 14 13 12 11 10

Contents

Preface

Pocket Guide to APA Style, 4th edition, is designed for students who need to write, document, and present papers in American Psychological Association style. This convenient and easy-to-use guide draws on the principles described in the corrected sixth edition of the *Publication Manual of the American Psychological Association* (2009). What sets *Pocket Guide to APA Style* apart from the lengthy *Publication Manual* is its overriding goal: This text presents the principles in a brief yet complete and easy-to-use manner. The guide is ideal for undergraduates who are working with APA style for the first time. Yet graduate students and working professionals will also appreciate its user-friendliness. To enhance its use, *Pocket Guide to APA Style* incorporates these helpful features:

- *Writing Scholarly Papers: An Overview* The introductory chapter of *Pocket Guide* describes basic researching and writing methods, serving as a brief review.

- *Manuscript Preparation* In one coherent chapter, *Pocket Guide* describes and illustrates all elements of an APA manuscript.

- *Editorial Style* In one convenient chapter, *Pocket Guide* explains APA guidelines for punctuation and mechanics (periods, quotation marks, capitalization, number style, and so on), general writing style (transitions, verb tense, and so on), and word choice (jargon, biased language, and so on).

- *Separate Documentation Chapters* For easy use, *Pocket Guide* provides separate chapters to explain reference-list entries for periodicals, books, audiovisual sources, and electronic sources.

- *Reference-List Entries and In-Text Citations* Chapters 4 to 8 include guidelines for documenting 60 kinds of sources, with 119 sample reference-list entries. These updated samples are followed by corresponding in-text citations.

- *Sample Papers* Two complete sample papers are included in *Pocket Guide,* one argumentative and one experimental; both include annotations related to manuscript form and issues of writing.

- *A Discussion of Plagiarism*   With its student focus, *Pocket Guide* includes a discussion of plagiarism and ways to avoid it.
- *Appendix*   Included in *Pocket Guide* is an appendix that describes effective ways to prepare poster presentations.

ACKNOWLEDGMENTS

My work on the fourth edition of *Pocket Guide* was pleasant and productive because of the supportive, knowledgeable staff at Wadsworth–Cengage Learning. I also thank MPS for their careful handling of the production work.

I am also indebted to the following people for their thoughtful reviews of earlier editions of *Pocket Guide to APA:*

Julie Burke, Guilford College

John Chapin, Pennsylvania State University

Larry Z. Daily, Shepherd University

Kathy Earnest, Northwestern Oklahoma State University

Cindy Giaimo-Ballard, University of La Verne

Sandra Petree, Northwestern Oklahoma State University

Finally, I wish to thank Judy, Jenny, Chris, and Kate for their encouragement.

R. P.

1   Writing Scholarly Papers

The research process is a complex combination of thinking, searching, reading, evaluating, writing, and revising. It is, in many ways, a highly personal process because writers approach research activities by drawing on different skills and past experiences. Yet researchers often follow a series of connected phases (which nonetheless occur in a different order for different people).

This chapter reviews, in a brief way, the common steps that most researchers go through; if you are an experienced researcher, you can use this chapter as a "refresher." If your research experiences are limited, consider each discussion carefully as you proceed with your work.

1a   Subject and Topic

Research begins with a subject. In some academic contexts, you may choose the subject yourself, usually with the instructor's approval. But in other contexts, you may be required to choose from a small number of topics or be assigned a topic with a predetermined focus.

GUIDELINES FOR ASSESSING GENERAL SUBJECTS

As you select potential subjects for your research (broad categories such as test anxiety, migrant education, the effects of divorce, and so on), keep in mind these practical and important principles:

- *Interest.* When possible, select a subject that interests you. Do not spend time researching a subject that does not make you curious.
- *Length.* Select a subject that can be adequately treated within the length requirements of the assignment. You may have to expand or reduce the scope of your subject to match these length constraints.
- *Materials.* Select a subject for which you can find materials of the kind identified in the assignment. Be aware that you can use libraries other than your own for your research and that the Internet provides access to a broad range of materials, both traditional and nontraditional.

- *Challenge.*   Select a subject that challenges you but that does not require technical or other specialized knowledge you may not have time to acquire.
- *Uniqueness.*   Select a subject that is not overused. Overly familiar subjects stimulate little interest, and materials are soon depleted.
- *Perspective.*   Select a subject you can approach in a fresh, interesting way. Readers will appreciate your efforts to examine subjects from new perspectives.

NARROW TOPIC

In most instances, you will need to narrow your large subject (test anxiety, for example) to a specific topic (test anxiety among middle school students) so that you can research selectively and address the issue in a focused way.

To discover ways to narrow a broad subject to a specific topic, skim general reference materials, paying particular attention to recurrent themes, details, and ideas. Then consider establishing a focus using selected strategies for limiting topics:

- *Time.*   Restrict the subject to a specific, manageable time span—for example, school violence in the 1990s.
- *Place.*   Restrict the subject to a specific location—for example, teen pregnancy in rural areas of the United States.
- *Special circumstance.*   Restrict the subject to a specific context or circumstance—for example, achievement testing for college admissions.
- *Specific population.*   Restrict the subject to address its effects on a selected group of people—for example, skin cancer among elderly people.

1b   Thesis Statements, Hypotheses, or Stated Objectives

To clarify the central goal of your writing, present your ideas in one of three alternative ways.

THESIS STATEMENT

A thesis statement, sometimes called a problem statement, is a declarative statement (usually one but sometimes two or more sentences) that clarifies your specific topic, presents your opinion of (not merely facts about) the topic, and incorporates qualifications or limitations necessary to understand your views.

> Although the effects of birth order are always evident to some degree, other variables also affect personality, intelligence, and socialization.

HYPOTHESIS

A hypothesis is a conjectural statement that guides an argument or investigation; it can be explored (and potentially proved or disproved) by examining data related to your topic. Conditional in nature, a hypothesis is assessed using available information.

> Students who delay work on major research projects until the last week are more likely to plagiarize than are students who begin their work early.

STATED OBJECTIVE

A stated objective is a brief, well-focused statement that describes a research paper that presents information. Unsubtle and not arguable, it must define the topic clearly and narrow the topic when necessary.

> I will share a brief history of polio in the United States, from early epidemics to the last American case.

1c   Research Goals

Although most research is prompted by specific academic or job-related requirements, you should also think broadly about the goals for your work, recognizing that research provides multifaceted learning experiences.

COURSE-RELATED GOALS

Course-related goals are broad in scope and establish the foundation of your research work.

- *Using the library.* Library-based research should take advantage of a full range of sources, as well as the electronic means to locate them (see pages 5–9).
- *Using the Internet for academic purposes.* Research requires that you learn to use the Internet selectively for

scholarly purposes, which involves learning to evaluate the credibility and value of online materials (see pages 10–11 and 11–13).

- *Assessing source materials.*   In a global way, research depends on evaluating materials critically to ensure that you use sources that credibly support your ideas (see pages 10–13).
- *Taking notes.*   Research requires you to record ideas and information from your sources carefully and completely so that you can use them appropriately in your writing (see pages 13–15).
- *Responding effectively to opposing views.*   Fair-minded research acknowledges and uses opposing views to maintain a balanced perspective.
- *Synthesizing ideas.*   Effective research blends information and ideas from a variety of sources, thereby creating a comprehensive presentation that is better or fairer or clearer than the presentation in individual sources.
- *Incorporating material into writing.*   Effective research leads to writing that incorporates ideas and information with clarity, accuracy, and style (see pages 20–24 and section 4f).
- *Citing sources accurately.*   Research requires you to give proper credit to the people whose ideas and information you have used; this technically focused process requires attention to detail (see Chapters 4–8).

PROFESSIONAL GOALS

Professional goals develop from the process of establishing a working knowledge in your field of study. As such, they focus on the acquisition of knowledge and specific skills.

- *Learning to use specific sources.*   Research in each discipline requires familiarity with the kinds of sources that are respected and commonly used.
- *Demonstrating discipline-specific knowledge.*   Research in each discipline builds upon accepted information that you must be able to incorporate fluently.
- *Using specialized formats.*   Each discipline's research incorporates unique formats that you must learn to follow.
- *Using specialized writing styles.*   Research in each discipline depends on specific stylistic patterns for presenting ideas and information.

PERSONAL GOALS

Personal goals concentrate on degrees of knowledge, improvement, sophistication, and experience. Although they are less easily quantified than goals matched to courses, they are also important.

- *Learning about a subject.* Exploring a subject through research improves your knowledge of your discipline.
- *Improving skills.* Conducting research gives you the opportunity not only to use your early research work but also to develop more sophisticated skills.
- *Expanding experiences.* Research work allows for varied kinds of personal growth.

1d Research Methods

Methods of research vary depending on the project, but most projects require multidimensional work with a variety of sources. To complete such projects, take advantage of a full range of strategies.

LIBRARY-BASED RESEARCH

Learn to use all of the features of your library, especially familiarizing yourself with the research areas that you will most commonly use:

- *Reference:* General source materials—dictionaries, fact books, encyclopedias, indexes, guides, bibliographies, and so on—that can guide your preliminary research (Most reference materials are now available in electronic form.)
- *Catalog (computer):* Computer clusters where you secure the records of library materials
- *Stacks:* Bookcases where print materials (bound periodicals, books, and so on) are stored according to a classification system
- *Current periodicals:* Recent copies of journals, magazines, and newspapers (Most periodicals are now available in electronic form.)
- *Government documents:* Printed materials from national, state, and local government departments and agencies—books, monographs, pamphlets, reports, and so on (Most government documents are available in electronic form through government websites.)

- *Microforms:* Microfilm and microfiche materials
- *Media:* Audiovisual sources—DVDs, Blu-rays, CDs, and so on
- *New books:* The area where new books are displayed before being placed in the general collection
- *Special collections:* The area where rare books, archival materials, and other special sources are located
- *Special libraries:* Discipline-specific collections that are housed in sublibraries

PERIODICAL DATABASES AND ONLINE CATALOGS

Periodical databases (online "indexes") allow you to gather technical information about—and frequently view full texts of—articles in journals, magazines, and newspapers. Online catalogs (electronic search systems) allow you to gather technical information about books, monographs, government documents, and other materials in the library's collection. Both periodical databases and online catalogs provide access to descriptive material about sources through keyword search techniques.

Keyword searching uses easily recognizable words and phrases (often in combination) to access sources. Computer systems search for keywords in titles, tables of contents, and other descriptive materials and then display "matches." To locate a broad range of materials, use alternative phrases (*collaborative learning, collaboration, team research,* and so on) as you conduct searches. Also explore Library of Congress listings, available online at most libraries, to discover unique category descriptions. For example, the Library of Congress system does not use the fairly conventional expression *medical ethics;* rather, its category notation is *medicine—moral and ethical aspects.*

Information About Periodicals

Most libraries now subscribe to a variety of periodical databases. These databases vary in design and format, but all provide a wide range of information about articles in journals, magazines, and newspapers. Most databases provide information about the following elements:

- *Article title:* Full title and subtitle of the article (listed first because some articles have no attributed authors)
- *Author:* Full name of the author (or authors)

- *Affiliation:* Professional affiliation (university, institution, and so on) of the author
- *Periodical title:* Title of the journal, magazine, or newspaper
- *Volume and issue number:* Volume (which indicates the number of years that a periodical has been published) and issue number (which refers to the specific issue in which the article appeared) for journals and magazines, but not for newspapers
- *Number of pages:* Total number of pages of the article (in the original print format); alternatively, the starting page of the article
- *Date:* Month/year, month/day/year, or season/year of publication
- *ISSN number:* The 8-digit International Standard Serial Number (ISSN) of the article
- *Abstract:* A short but detailed overview of the article, emphasizing key ideas and briefly explaining procedures
- *Language:* The language in which the article is written (English, Japanese, Farsi, and so on)
- *Document type:* A brief description of the article (feature article, journal article, review, and so on)
- *Classification:* The article's subclassification within the discipline (child psychology, educational psychology, cognitive psychology, and so on)
- *Subjects or Keywords:* Subjects or specific phrases in the article (medical ethics, juvenile delinquency, test anxiety, and so on)
- *Publisher or source:* A description of the periodical (periodical, peer-reviewed journal, and so on)
- *DOI:* The Digital Object Identifier (DOI) assigned to the article
- *Formats for articles:* Formats available for selected articles: HTML, PDF, summary, abstract (see page 9)
- *Database:* The name of the database that provides the digital record
- *Options:* Choices for using the database record for the source (Save, Print, E-mail, and so on)

In addition to these common elements, individual databases provide other detailed information: the author's e-mail address, the publication year, the database access number, the country of publication, the database identification number, the document URL, the number of references, the word count, the research techniques (tests and measures, age of research subjects, methodology), the publication history (date submitted, revised, and accepted), and the copyright.

You may never need all of the information provided in a database listing, but reviewing the full range of material will allow you to assess a source before retrieving it.

Information About Books (and Other Library-Based Materials)

Online catalogs provide standardized information about each source in the library's collection:

- *Author:*   Full name of the author (or authors)
- *Title:*   Full title of the source, including subtitles
- *Facts of publication:*   City, publisher, and copyright date
- *ISBN:*   The 10-digit International Standard Book Number (ISBN) if the source is a book
- *Technical description:*   Specific features—edition, number of pages, use of illustrations, book size, and so on
- *Format:*   Description of the source (book, book with CD, book with audiotape, and so on)
- *Subject classification:*   Library of Congress classification, both primary and secondary
- *Notes:*   Descriptions of special features (bibliography, index, appendices, and so on)
- *Location:*   Location of the source in the library's collection (general collection, special collection, or specialty library)
- *Call number:*   Classification number assigned to the source (indicating where the source is located in the collection)
- *Number of items:*   Number of items (three volumes, one volume with CD-ROM, and so on), if more than one exists
- *Status:*   Information on whether the source is checked out, on reserve, on loan, and so on
- *Options:*   Choices for using the online catalog record for the source (Save, Print, E-mail, Add to List, and so on)

Many online catalogs provide links to websites like *Google Books*, which provide other kinds of information: reviews from readers, sources for buying books (Amazon.com, BarnesandNoble.com, and so on), a list of other books that refer to the source, other available editions, the table of contents, the length, the cost, and so on.

Format Options (Within a Periodical Database)

- *HTML:*   HyperText Markup Language. A digitized version of the article available on a website
- *PDF:*   Portable Document Format. A page-by-page scanned image of the article as it appeared in the printed periodical, available as a single file

---

INTERNET-BASED RESEARCH

Internet research may lead you to a scholarly project (a university-based, scholarly site that provides a wide range of materials—such as full-text books, research data, and visual materials), an information database (a site that offers statistical information from governmental agencies, research institutions, or nonprofit corporations), or a website (a site designed to share information or ideas, forward a political agenda, promote a product, or advocate a position).

To navigate an Internet site successfully and to gather crucial information for a reference-list entry, learn about the key elements of an Internet home page:

- *Electronic address (URL):*   Uniform Resource Locator—the combination of elements that locates the source (For example, http://www.aagpgpa.org is the URL for the website of the American Association for Geriatric Psychology)
- *Official title:*   Title and subtitle of the site
- *Author, host, editor, or web master:*   Person (or people) responsible for developing and maintaining the site
- *Affiliation or sponsorship:*   Person, group, organization, or agency that develops and maintains the material on the site
- *Location:*   Place (city, school, organization, agency, and so on) from which the site originates
- *Posting date or update:*   Date on which the site was first posted or most recently updated (revised)
- *"About This Site":*   Description of how the site was developed, a rationale for it, or information about those involved with the site
- *Site directory:*   Electronic table of contents for the site

1e Evaluating Sources

Because not all sources are equally useful, you should analyze them and select the ones best suited to your research. This ongoing process requires continued assessments and reassessments.

PRINT SOURCES (AND THEIR ELECTRONIC COUNTERPARTS)

Print sources—journals, magazines, newspapers, books, and so on—have traditionally been the mainstay of most research; today, many of these sources are also available in electronic formats. Whether available in print or available in an alternative electronic format, these sources are the easiest to evaluate because of their familiarity.

- *Author's credentials.* Determine whether an author's academic degrees, scholarly training, affiliations, or other published work establish his or her authority.
- *Appropriate focus.* Determine whether the source addresses the topic in a way that matches your emphasis. Consider literature reviews to establish scholarly context and empirical studies to incorporate recent primary research.
- *Sufficient coverage.* Determine whether the source sufficiently covers the topic by examining its table of contents, reviewing the index, and skimming a portion of the text.
- *Respected periodicals.* Generally, use journals with strong organizational affiliations; furthermore, note that peer-reviewed journals (those that publish works only after they have been recommended by a panel of expert reviewers) offer more credibility than non-peer-reviewed journals. Choose specialized, rather than general-interest, magazines. Choose major newspapers for topics of international or national importance, but choose regional or local newspapers for issues of regional or local importance.
- *Reputable publisher.* University, academic, or trade presses publish most of the books you will use, which generally ensures their credibility. Note also that publishers often specialize in books related to particular subjects.
- *Publication date.* For many topics, sources more than 5 or 10 years old have limited value. However, consider creating a historical context by using older sources.

- *Useful supplementary materials.*   Look for in-text illustrations, tables, charts, graphs, diagrams, bibliographies, case studies, or collections of additional readings.
- *Appropriate writing style.*   Skim a potential source to see how it is developed (with facts, examples, description, or narration); also consider whether the author's style is varied, clear, and persuasive.

INTERNET SOURCES

Although Internet sources provide a fascinating array of materials, some of the material posted on the Internet has not been subjected to scholarly review and is, therefore, not necessarily credible. As a result, you should use only Internet sources that meet important evaluative criteria:

- *Author, editor, host, or web master's credentials.*   A website may or may not have an author, editor, host, or web master. If it does, explore the site for information about his or her qualifications to discuss the topic.
- *Appropriate focus.*   Skim the website to see whether its focus is suitable for your topic. Sometimes the site's title makes the focus clear; at other times, an entire site has a general focus, but its internal links allow you to locate material on narrower aspects of the larger subject.
- *Sufficient coverage.*   Review documents on the website to see whether the coverage is thorough enough for your purposes.
- *Domains.*   Examine the website's electronic address (URL) to see how the site is registered with the Internet Corporation for Assigned Names and Numbers (ICANN). The following common "top-level domains" provide useful clues about a site's focus and function:

.com	A commercial site. The primary function of a commercial site is to make money.
.edu	A site affiliated with an educational institution. These sites may be posted by the school or by an individual affiliated with the institution.
.gov	A government site. These sites present trustworthy information (statistics, facts, reports), but the interpretive materials may be less useful.
.mil	A military site. The technical information on these sites is consistently useful, but interpretive material tends to justify a single, pro-military position.

.museum   A site for a museum. Because museums can be either nonprofit or for-profit institutions, consider the purpose that the particular museum serves.

.org   An organizational site. Because organizations seek to advance political, social, financial, educational, and other specific agendas, review these materials with care.

- *Possible biases.* Do not automatically discount or overvalue what you find on any particular kind of website. Rather, consider the biases that influence how the information on a site is presented and interpreted.

- *Affiliation or sponsorship.* Examine the website to see whether it has an affiliation or a sponsorship beyond what is suggested by the site's domain.

- *Posting or revision date.* Identify the date of original posting or the date on which information was updated. Because currency is one of the benefits of Internet sources, look for websites that provide recent information.

- *Documentation.* Review Internet materials to see how thoroughly authors have documented their information. If facts, statistics, and other technical information are not documented appropriately, the information may be questionable.

- *Links to or from other sites.* Consider the "referral quality" that Internet links provide.

- *Appropriate writing style.* Skim the website to see how it is written. All sources do not, of course, have to be written in the same style, but it is an issue worth considering when you evaluate a source.

AUDIOVISUAL SOURCES

Because of the range of audiovisual sources available, use specific criteria to assess each kind of source individually. Many of the techniques employed for evaluating these sources correspond to those used for print and Internet sources.

- *Lectures and speeches.* Use criteria similar to those for print sources: speaker, relationship to your topic, coverage, sponsoring group or organization, and date.

- *Works of art, photographs, cartoons, and recordings.* Because these sources are used primarily to create interest in most research papers, consider how well the image or performance illuminates your topic.

- *Maps, graphs, tables, and charts.* Evaluate these visual sources the same way as traditional print sources.
- *Motion pictures, television shows, and radio programs.* When these sources serve informative purposes, evaluate them as you would assess print sources; when they are used creatively, evaluate them using the same criteria you would apply to other creative audiovisual forms.

COMBINATIONS OF SOURCES

Although you must first evaluate your sources individually—whether they are print, Internet, or audiovisual—your goal is to gather a set of high-quality sources that together provide a balanced treatment of your topic. Consider these issues:

- *Alternative perspectives.* Taken collectively, does the work of your authors provide a range of perspectives—academic and popular, liberal and conservative, theoretical and practical, current and traditional?
- *Varied publication, release, or distribution dates.* Does your group of sources represent the information, ideas, and interpretations of different periods, when appropriate?
- *Different approaches to the topic.* In combination, your sources should range from the technical (including facts and statistics) to the interpretive (providing commentary and assessments). Also consider literature reviews for secondary analyses and empirical studies for primary research.
- *Diversity of sources.* Incorporate in your work a wide range of sources—periodicals, books, electronic sources, and audiovisual sources—to ensure that you have taken advantage of the strengths of each kind of source. Be aware, however, that in some instances your research must focus on selected kinds of sources.

Evaluating sources is an inexact process. No matter how carefully you review materials, some may later prove unhelpful. Yet early efforts to evaluate sources generally enhance the focus and efficiency of later, more comprehensive work, such as reading and taking notes from the sources.

1f Note-Taking

Note-taking is an individualized process, because different researchers prefer different methods for recording information and ideas from sources. However, all note-taking should be meticulous and consistent, both to avoid plagiarism and to simplify the subsequent writing of the paper. Consider alternative methods for note-taking and remember that note-taking must be complete, consistent, matched to the kind of material being used, and honest.

Before taking notes from a source, create a complete and accurate entry for the reference list. See Chapters 4–8 for guidelines and samples.

METHODS OF NOTE-TAKING

Begin your note-taking by analyzing each note-taking system and choosing the one best suited to your specific project, library facilities, work habits, and instructor's expectations.

- *Note cards.* Note cards are easy to handle and to rearrange during planning stages, but they hold only limited amounts of information.
- *Paper.* Paper is easy to handle and has sufficient room for copious notes, but notes on paper are difficult to organize during planning stages.
- *Computers.* Notes on computers do not have to be retyped during the writing process and can be printed multiple times, but on-site note-taking with computers is sometimes awkward.
- *Photocopies and printed texts.* Photocopied and printed materials do not have to be recopied, and you can write on them. However, photocopying and printing can be expensive.

COMPLETE INFORMATION

Record complete identifying information with each separate note to avoid having to return to a source at a later, and potentially less convenient, time.

- *Author's name.* Record the author's last name (and first initial, if necessary for clarity); for multiauthor sources, record only as many names as are necessary for clarity.
- *Title.* Record only important words from titles but use italics or quotation marks as appropriate.
- *Category notation.* Provide a brief descriptive term to indicate the idea or subtopic that the information supports.
- *Page numbers.* Record the page number(s) from which you gathered information. If material comes from several

pages, indicate where the page break occurs. (A double slash [//] is a useful way to indicate a page break.) Also indicate when an electronic source does not include pages.

CONSISTENT FORMAT

Record notes in a consistent format to avoid confusion at later stages of research and writing.

- *Placement of information.* Establish a consistent pattern for placing information so that nothing is omitted accidentally.
- *Abbreviations.* Use abbreviations selectively to save time and space; however, use only standard abbreviations to avoid possible confusion later.
- *Notations.* Note anything unique about the source (for example, no page numbers in a pamphlet or an especially good chart).

KINDS OF NOTES

Four common kinds of notes serve most research purposes. Choose among these kinds of note-taking patterns depending on the sources you use and the kinds of materials they include.

- *Facts.* A fact note records technical information—names, dates, percentages—in minimal form. Record words, phrases, and information in a simple outline or list format and double-check the information for accuracy.
- *Summaries.* A summary note presents the substance of a passage in condensed form. After reading original material carefully, write a summary without looking at the original; this will ensure that the phrasing is yours, not the author's. Double-check the summary note to make sure that your wording is distinct from the original.
- *Paraphrases.* A paraphrase note restates ideas from a passage in your own words, using approximately the same number of words. Write a paraphrase without looking at the original and then double-check the note to ensure that the phrasing is yours.
- *Quotations.* A quotation note reproduces a writer's words exactly. Double-check the quotation note against the original; the copy must be an exact transcription of the original wording, capitalization, punctuation, and other elements.

1g Plagiarism

Plagiarism, from the Latin word for kidnapping, is the use of someone else's words, ideas, or line of thought without acknowledgment. In its most extreme form, plagiarism involves submitting someone else's completed work as your own. A less extreme but equally unacceptable form involves copying and pasting entire segments of another writer's work into your own writing. A third form of plagiarism involves carelessly or inadvertently blending elements (words, phrases, ideas) of a writer's work into your own.

- *Whole-paper plagiarism.* This kind of plagiarism is easily discovered. Through experiences with students in class, instructors learn what students are interested in and how they express themselves (sentence patterns, diction, and technical fluency).

- *Copy-and-paste plagiarism.* This kind of plagiarism is also easy to detect because of abrupt shifts in sentence sophistication, diction, or technical fluency.

- *Careless plagiarism.* This form of plagiarism is evident when distinct material is unquoted or when specialized information (dates, percentages, and other facts) is not acknowledged. Even when this is carelessly or inadvertently done, the writer is still at fault for dishonest work, and the paper is still unacceptable.

In all of its forms, plagiarism is academically dishonest and unacceptable, and the penalties for its practice range from failing individual papers or projects to failing courses to being dismissed from college to having degrees revoked. The seriousness of plagiarism cannot be ignored, so you must make a conscious effort to avoid this practice. To avoid plagiarizing, learn to recognize the distinctive content and expression in source materials and take accurate, carefully punctuated, and documented notes.

COMMON KNOWLEDGE

Some kinds of information—facts and interpretations—are known by many people and are consequently described as common knowledge. That Alzheimer's disease is the leading cause of dementia in elderly people is widely known, as is the more interpretive information that Alzheimer's disease is best treated by a combination of drug and psychiatric therapies. But common knowledge extends beyond these very general types of information to include more specific information within a field of study. In medical studies, for example, it is widely known that Prozac is the trade name for fluoxetine hydrochloride; in education, a commonly acknowledged interpretation is that high scores on standardized tests do not uniformly predict academic success. Documenting these facts, beliefs, and interpretations in a paper would be unnecessary because they are commonly known in their areas of study, even though you might have discovered them for the first time.

When you are researching an unfamiliar subject, distinguishing common knowledge that does not require documentation from special knowledge that does require documentation is sometimes difficult. The following guidelines may help.

What constitutes common knowledge

- *Historical facts* (names, dates, and general interpretations) that appear in many general reference books. For example, Sigmund Freud's most influential work, *The Interpretation of Dreams*, was published in 1899.

- *General observations and opinions* that are shared by many people. For example, it is a general observation that children learn by actively doing, rather than passively listening, and it is a commonly held opinion that reading, writing, and arithmetic are the basic skills that elementary school students should acquire.

- *Unacknowledged information* that appears in multiple sources. For example, it is common knowledge that the earth's population is roughly 6.8 billion people and that an *IQ* is a gauge of intelligence determined by a person's knowledge in relation to his or her age.

If a piece of information does not meet these guidelines or if you are uncertain about whether it is common knowledge, always document the material.

SPECIAL QUALITIES OF SOURCE MATERIALS

A more difficult problem than identifying common knowledge involves using an author's words and ideas improperly. Improper use often results from careless summarizing and paraphrasing. To use source materials without plagiarizing, learn to recognize their distinctive qualities.

Special qualities of sources

- *Distinctive prose style:* The author's chosen words, phrases, and sentence patterns
- *Original facts:* Results of the author's personal research

- *Personal interpretations of information:* The author's individual evaluation of his or her information
- *Original ideas:* Ideas that are unique to a particular author

As you work with sources, be aware of these distinguishing qualities and make certain that you do not incorporate into your writing the prose (word choices and sentence structures), original research, interpretations, or ideas of others without giving proper credit.

Consider, for example, the following paragraphs from Appleby, Hunt, and Jacob's (1994) *Telling the Truth About History* (New York, NY: Norton):

> Interest in this new research in social history can be partly explained by the personal backgrounds of the cohort of historians who undertook the task of writing history from the bottom up. They entered higher education with the post-*Sputnik* expansion of the 1950s and 1960s, when the number of new Ph.D.s in history nearly quadrupled. Since many of them were children and grandchildren of immigrants, they had a personal incentive for turning the writing of their dissertations into a movement of memory recovery. Others were black or female and similarly prompted to find ways to make the historically inarticulate speak. While the number of male Ph.D.s in history ebbed and flowed with the vicissitudes of the job market, the number of new female Ph.D.s in history steadily increased from 11 percent (29) in 1950 to 13 percent (137) in 1970 and finally to 37 percent (192) in 1989.
>
> Although ethnicity is harder to locate in the records, the GI Bill was clearly effective in bringing the children of working-class families into the middle-class educational mainstream. This was the thin end of a democratizing wedge prying open higher education in the United States. Never before had so many people in any society earned so many higher degrees. Important as their numbers were, the change in perspective these academics brought to their disciplines has made the qualitative changes even more impressive. Suddenly graduate students with strange, unpronounceable surnames, with Brooklyn accents and different skin colors, appeared in the venerable ivy-covered buildings that epitomized elite schooling.

Now look at the following examples of faulty and acceptable summaries and paraphrases. Questionable phrases in the faulty samples are underlined.

Faulty summary: plagiarism likely

Appleby, Hunt, Jacob   historians' backgrounds

-- A historian's focus is _partially explained_ by his or her _personal background_.

-- Because of their experiences, _they have a personal incentive_ for looking at history in new ways.

-- Large numbers were important, but the change in viewpoint _made the qualitative changes even more impressive_.

pp. 146–147

Acceptable summary: plagiarism unlikely

Appleby, Hunt, Jacob   historians' backgrounds

-- A historian's focus and interpretations are personal.

-- For personal reasons, not always stated, people examine the facts of history from different perspectives.

-- Large numbers were important, but the change in viewpoint "made the qualitative changes even more impressive."

pp. 146–147

Faulty paraphrase: plagiarism likely

Appleby, Hunt, Jacob   the GI Bill

-- _Even though ethnic background is not easily found_ in the statistics, the GI Bill consistently helped students from _low-income families enter the middle-class educational system_. This was how _democracy started forcing open college education in America._

pp. 146–147

Acceptable paraphrase: plagiarism unlikely

Appleby, Hunt, Jacob   the GI Bill

-- Because of the GI Bill, even poor people could attend
college. For the first time, education was accessible
to everyone, which is truly democracy in action. The GI
Bill was "the thin end of a democratizing wedge prying
open higher education."

pp. 146–147

1h   Planning

After gathering information, organizing the research paper
is an exciting stage because you are ready to bring ideas together in a clear and logical form.

REVIEWING NOTES

Begin by rereading the assignment sheet to reexamine the
principles guiding your work. Then review your notes to see
the range of materials you have collected and to identify connections among ideas.

THESIS STATEMENT OR STATED OBJECTIVE

After rereading your notes, revise the thesis statement, hypothesis, or objective so that it accurately represents the paper you plan to write. Is the topic clear? Does it express your
current (more informed) view? Does it contain appropriate
qualifications and limitations? Is it worded effectively?

AN INFORMAL OUTLINE

An informal outline is a structural plan prepared for your
own use. Arrange information in logical ways using numbers,
arrows, dashes, dots, or other convenient symbols to indicate the order for presentation and the relative importance
of ideas.

Using the major headings from the informal outline, sort
your notes. If a note fits into more than one group, place it in
the most appropriate group and place a cross-reference note

(for example, "See Parker quotation, p. 219—in *Childhood*") in each of the other appropriate groups.

A FORMAL OUTLINE

If you choose to develop a formal outline, adhere to the following conventions to establish divisions within the outline:

- *Major topics.* Use uppercase Roman numerals (*I, II, III*) to indicate major topics.
- *Subdivisions.* Use uppercase letters (*A, B, C*) to indicate subdivisions of major topics.
- *Clarifications.* Use Arabic numerals (*1, 2, 3*) to indicate clarifications of subdivisions—usually examples, supporting facts, and so on.
- *Details.* Use lowercase letters (*a, b, c*) to indicate details used to describe the examples.

In addition, observe the following conventions:

- Use parallel form throughout. Use words and phrases to develop a topic outline or use full sentences to develop a sentence outline.
- Include only one idea in each entry. Subdivide entries that contain two or more ideas.
- Include at least two entries at each sublevel.
- Indent headings of the same level the same number of spaces from the margin.

1i Writing Strategies

Because incorporating research materials and using in-text documentation extend the time it takes to write a paper, allow ample time to write the draft of your paper. Consider both the general and special circumstances that affect the process of writing and revising any paper, as well as those issues that relate specifically to writing and revising a documented paper.

GENERAL STRATEGIES FOR DRAFTING A PAPER

Because the research paper is in many ways like all other papers, keep these general writing strategies in mind:

- *Gather materials.* Collect planning materials and writing supplies before you begin writing. Working consistently in the same location is also helpful because all materials are there when you wish to write.

- *Work from an outline.* Following an outline, whether informal or formal, develop paragraphs and sections; write troublesome sections late in the process.

- *Keep the paper's purpose in mind.* Arrange and develop only those ideas that your outline indicates are important.

- *Develop the paper "promised" by the thesis, hypothesis, or objective.* Incorporate only the ideas and information that support your thesis, hypothesis, or objective.

- *Attend to technical matters later.* Concentrate on developing your ideas and presenting your information; you can revise the paper later to correct any technical errors.

- *Rethink troublesome sections.* When sections are difficult to write, reconsider their importance or means of development. Revise the outline if necessary.

- *Reread as you write.* Reread early sections as you write to maintain a consistent tone and style.

- *Write alternative sections.* Write several versions of troublesome sections and then choose the best one.

- *Take periodic breaks.* Get away from your work for short periods so that you can maintain a fresh perspective and attain objectivity.

STRATEGIES FOR DRAFTING A RESEARCH PAPER

Because the research paper has its own distinct qualities and demands, keep these special strategies in mind:

- *Allow ample time.* Give yourself plenty of time to write a research paper; its length and complexity will affect the speed at which you work.

- *Think about sections, not paragraphs.* Think of the paper in terms of sections, not paragraphs. Large sections will probably contain several paragraphs.

- *Use transitions.* Although headings can divide your work into logical segments, use well-chosen transitional words to signal shifts between elements of the paper.

- *Attend to technical language.* Define technical terms carefully to clarify ideas.

- *Incorporate notes smoothly.* Use research materials to support and illustrate, not dominate, your discussion.

- *Document carefully.* Use in-text citations (notes in parentheses) to acknowledge the sources of your ideas and information (see Chapter 4, "Preparing the Reference List and In-Text Citations").

QUESTIONS FOR REVISING CONTENT

Examine the paper's content for clarity, coherence, and completeness. Consider these issues:

- *Title, introduction, headings, conclusion.* Are your title, introduction, headings, and conclusion well matched to the tone and purpose of the paper?
- *Thesis (hypothesis) and development.* Does the thesis accurately represent your current view on the topic, and does the paper develop that idea?
- *Support for thesis.* Do research materials effectively support the paper's thesis? Have you eliminated materials (details, sentences, even paragraphs) that do not directly support your thesis?
- *Organization.* Does your organizational pattern present your ideas logically and effectively?
- *Use of materials.* Have you incorporated a range of materials to develop your ideas in a varied, interesting, and complete way?
- *Balance among sections.* Are the sections of the paper balanced in length and emphasis?
- *Balance among sources.* Have you used a variety of sources to support your ideas?
- *Transitions.* Do transitions connect sections of the paper in a coherent way?

QUESTIONS FOR REVISING STYLE

Achieving coherent, balanced, well-developed content is one aspect of revision. Another consideration is achieving a clear and compelling presentation. Refine the paper's style, keeping these issues in mind:

- *Tone.* Is the tone suited to the topic and presentation?
- *Sentences.* Are the sentences varied in both length and type? Have you written active, rather than passive, sentences?

- *Diction.* Are the word choices vivid, accurate, and appropriate?
- *Introduction of research materials.* Have you introduced research materials (facts, summaries, paraphrases, and quotations) with variety and clarity?

QUESTIONS FOR REVISING TECHNICAL MATTERS

Technical revision focuses on grammar, usage, punctuation, mechanics, spelling, and manuscript form. After revising content and style, consider technical revisions to make the presentation correct and precise, giving particular attention to issues related to documentation:

- *Grammar.* Are your sentences complete? Do pronouns agree with nouns, and verbs with subjects? Have you worked to avoid errors that you commonly make?
- *Punctuation and mechanics.* Have you double-checked your punctuation? Have you spell-checked the paper? Have you used quotation marks and italics correctly?
- *Quotations.* Are quotations presented correctly, depending on their length or emphasis?
- *In-text citations.* Are in-text citations placed appropriately and punctuated correctly?
- *Reference list.* Have you listed only the sources actually used in the paper? Is your list alphabetized correctly? Is each entry complete and correct?
- *Manuscript guidelines.* Are margins, line spacing, and paging correct? Does the paper include all necessary elements?

2   Preparing APA Manuscripts

APA style guidelines for manuscript preparation ensure that manuscripts follow uniform standards and, as a result, present the elements of papers in a generally understood way.

2a   Parts of the Manuscript

A manuscript for an APA paper can contain as many as eight separate parts: the title page (with author note), abstract, text of the paper, reference list, footnotes, tables, figures (with figure captions), and appendices. Not all papers have all of these elements, but when they do, they are arranged in this order.

The first part of this chapter addresses the specific requirements for preparing each element of an APA paper. The last part provides general manuscript guidelines.

TITLE PAGE

The first page of a manuscript is the title page (see pages 117 and 127 for samples), composed of the following elements:

- *Running head with paging.* As the first line of the title page, supply a running head, a shortened version of the paper's title with the page number. Full instructions for creating the running head appear on page 35, and samples appear on pages 117–137.

- *Title.* Center the title and use headline-style capitalization (see page 48). A good title is descriptive, clarifying both the topic and the perspective of the paper; when possible, the title should create interest through effective wording. APA recommends that titles be no more than 12 words long (a title of this length generally fits on a single line). If the title is longer than one line, divide it logically and center both lines.

- *Author's name.* Two lines below the title, include your name (centered and capitalized normally); APA recommends using your first name and middle initial(s) for additional clarity. Two lines below, list your affiliation; normally, this is your school's name, but you can list the city and state where you live. (Some instructors may also ask that you include the title of the course for which you wrote the paper.)

- *Author note.* At least four spaces below the affiliation, type the phrase *Author note* (not italicized but centered), followed by a series of clarifying paragraphs: (a) the first paragraph identifies the author's departmental and university affiliation; (b) the second paragraph identifies changes in affiliation, if any; (c) the third paragraph provides acknowledgments, preceded by any necessary disclaimers or explanations of special circumstances; and (d) the fourth paragraph presents the author's contact information. Use separate, indented, double-spaced paragraphs for each element.

- *NOTE:* Student work—papers for classes, theses, and dissertations—typically does not require an author note.

Parts of an APA Paper

- *Title page.* The opening page incorporates information to label the pages of the paper, highlights the title of the paper, and provides identifying information about the author. An author note may be included at the bottom of the title page.

- *Abstract.* This paragraph presents a brief but detailed overview of the paper, emphasizing key ideas and research procedures.

- *Text.* The text of an argumentative paper or review contains an introduction, body, and conclusion; it is frequently divided using headings that describe the main elements of the discussion. The text of a research study contains an introduction to the problem, an explanation of methodology, a summary of results, and a discussion of the implications of the study.

- *Reference list.* The alphabetically arranged reference list provides publication information for the sources used in the paper.

- *Footnotes.* Content footnotes include clarifying discussions and explanations that might disrupt the flow of the paper. Alternatively, footnotes may be incorporated within the text of the paper using the footnote function of your word processor.

- *Tables.* Numbered tables include technical data in easily interpreted and comparable forms. References within the paper correspond to tables that appear on separate pages near the end of the manuscript.

Parts of an APA Paper

- *Figures.* Visual images to support ideas in a paper (drawings, graphs, photographs, maps, and so on) appear as numbered figures. References within the paper correspond to the captioned figures that appear on separate pages at the end of the manuscript.

- *Appendices.* Appendices provide supplementary information that supports the ideas in the paper but would be awkward to include in the paper itself.

ABSTRACT

The abstract (the second page of the manuscript) follows the title page and provides a brief description of the major ideas in the paper (see page 117 for a sample). Because it must summarize the full range of ideas and information in the paper, it is generally written after the manuscript is complete. It must adhere to the following guidelines:

- *Heading.* Three lines below the running head, type the word *Abstract*, centered but not italicized. Two lines below, begin the paragraph.

- *Format.* The abstract is a single, unindented, double-spaced paragraph.

- *Length.* Abstracts in APA journals are typically 150 to 250 words.

- *Concision.* To save space in the abstract, use standard abbreviations (*AMA*, rather than *American Medical Association*); use digits for all numbers except those that begin sentences; and use active, rather than passive, sentences.

- *Content.* In the opening sentence, describe the topic or problem addressed in the paper. Use the remaining words in the paragraph to clarify methodology (for a research study), to identify four or five major ideas, and to explain results or conclusions. If a paper is lengthy and multifaceted, describe only the most important elements.

- *Keywords.* You may include a keyword list with your abstract. Two lines below the abstract, indent, type *Keywords* (italicized, followed by a colon), and provide a brief list of words that best describe the content of your paper.

TEXT

The text of the paper begins on the third page of the manuscript (see pages 118–124 for sample pages). The running head, as always, appears on the top line. Three lines below, center the title, with headline-style capitalization but without special print features (bold, italics, underlining, change in font size, or quotation marks). Two lines below the title, the double-spaced paper begins. The organization of the body of the paper depends on the paper's focus.

An Argumentative Paper, Review, or Meta-Analysis

- *Introduction.*   In this unlabeled section, define, describe, or clarify the topic (problem) and place it within its historical or scholarly context. Present a thesis (a statement of your topic and opinion) to clarify the purpose of your work.

- *Body.*   Examine the facets of the topic (problem) by reviewing current research: evaluate the positions held by others; analyze current data; assess the interpretations of others; synthesize the information and ideas found in other people's work. Use headings and subheadings throughout this section to direct readers through your argument.

- *Conclusion.*   Summarize key points, draw connections among important ideas, and reiterate your thesis.

- *Reference list.*   This labeled section provides a list of sources cited in the paper (see Chapter 4).

- *Additional materials.*   As appropriate, include the following labeled sections: footnotes, tables, figures, and appendices.

A Research Study

- *Introduction.*   In this unlabeled section, describe the problem, state your hypothesis, and describe your research methodology. Consider the importance of the problem and the ways in which the study addresses the problem. Present a historical or contextual discussion of what scholars have written, acknowledging alternative perspectives and differing interpretations.

A Research Study

- *Method.*   This labeled section should be further divided into labeled subsections that describe participants in the study (and procedures for selecting them), materials used (ranging from standard equipment to custom materials), and procedures (the step-by-step process for conducting the research).

- *Results.*   This labeled section summarizes the gathered information. It should be further subdivided into labeled subsections that analyze information that is illustrated by tables, figures, and other statistical material.

- *Discussion.*   This labeled section opens with an assertion about the correlation of your data with your original hypothesis. The remaining discussion can address how your findings relate to the work of others, what qualifications are necessary, the value of alternative interpretations, or what conclusions you have reached. End the discussion by commenting on the significance of your research results.

- *Reference list.*   This labeled section provides a list of sources cited in the paper (see Chapter 4).

- *Additional materials.*   As appropriate, include the following labeled sections: footnotes, tables, figures, and appendices.

REFERENCE LIST

The reference list, which continues the paging of the entire manuscript, provides publishing information for all sources used in the paper (see pages 125 and 134 for samples). Chapter 4 provides a comprehensive discussion of the information required in reference-list entries and the format for presenting the information. Chapters 5 to 8 provide explanations of 60 kinds of sources, with 121 separate samples for preparing reference-list entries for periodicals, books and other print materials, audiovisual sources, and electronic sources. Each entry appears with a corresponding in-text citation.

FOOTNOTES

Content footnotes allow writers to provide additional discussion or clarification that, although important, might disrupt the flow of a paper.

Footnotes follow these guidelines for placement and presentation:

- *Heading.* Three lines below the running head, type the word *Footnotes*, centered but not italicized.
- *Order of notes.* On the footnote page, footnotes appear in the order in which references appear in the text of the paper. Double-check the numbering.
- *Format.* Footnotes are typed in paragraph style, double-spaced, with the first line indented and subsequent lines aligned at the left margin. "Tab" once (for a five-space indentation), insert the superscript number, and type the footnote. No space separates the note number from the first letter of the first word of the footnote.
- *Paging.* Footnotes appear on a new page. Multiple footnotes are placed on the same page, with no additional space between the notes.
- *NOTE:* Alternately, footnotes may be incorporated within the text of the paper using the footnote function of your word-processing program.

Placing Note Numbers in the Paper

- *In-text notes.* Footnotes are numbered sequentially throughout a paper.
- *Placement of in-text note numbers.* In the text of the paper, refer to a content note by using a superscript number (a number placed above the line, like this[1]) without additional space. Word-processing programs allow you to achieve this result by using the "Font" feature.
- *Punctuation and note numbers.* Note numbers follow all punctuation marks, except dashes and parentheses. A note number precedes the dash[2]—without additional space. A note number may appear within parentheses (when it refers only to materials with the parentheses[3]). If the note refers to the entire sentence, however, it follows the parentheses (as in this sample).[4]

TABLES

Because tables present labeled information in columns (vertical elements) and rows (horizontal elements) for easy interpretation or comparison, they are helpful additions to papers that use technical data (see page 136 for a sample). Within the text of the paper, a reference (for example, "see Table 1") directs readers to tables using numerals (which correspond to tables presented near the end of the manuscript). Tables are prepared on separate pages and are presented according to these principles:

- *Table identification.*   Three lines below the running head (flush with the left margin), type the word *Table* and the table's Arabic numeral (Table 3, Table 4), not italicized.

- *Title of the table.*   Two spaces below the table heading, also flush left, type the title of the table in italics, with headline-style capitalization. One line below, insert a horizontal, 1-point rule (line); use the graphics or "Insert" feature of your word-processing program to create this element.

- *Column headings.*   Capitalize only the first letter of the first word of column headings, and center the column heading over the information in each column. One line below the column headings, insert a horizontal rule.

- *Parallel information and style.*   To maintain consistency, headings should appear in parallel grammatical forms (all nouns, all gerunds, and so on), and numbers should appear in similar style (with decimals, rounded to whole numbers, and so on).

- *Spacing.*   The primary elements of tables are single-spaced, and columns should be separated by at least three spaces for visual clarity. However, table notes (general and specific) are double-spaced.

- *Repeated information.*   If information from a table extends beyond one page, repeat the column headings.

- *Table notes (general).*   To provide an explanation of an entire table, include a general note. One line below the body of the table, insert a horizontal rule. Below the rule, type the word *Note* (italicized and flush with the left margin) followed by a period; after one space, type the text of the note, which remains flush left if it extends beyond one line. Place a period at the end of the note, even if it is not a complete sentence. These notes are double-spaced.

- *Table notes (specific).*   To provide an explanation of a specific element within a table, include a specific note. Within the table, insert a superscript lowercase letter—like this[a]—following the element. One line below the body of the table, insert a horizontal rule. Below the horizontal rule and flush with the left margin, insert the corresponding superscript lowercase letter, followed by the explanation. Place a period at the end of the note, even if it is not a complete sentence. If a table also has a general table note, it appears first; the specific table note appears on the line below. If a table has more than one specific note, they continue on the same line, separated by one space. These notes are double-spaced.

- *Paging.*   Each table must begin on a new page.

FIGURES

Figures are visual elements—drawings, graphs, photographs, maps, and so on—that cannot be reproduced by traditional typing (see page 136 for a sample). Each figure is numbered as it is used in the paper; original figures then appear on separate pages at the end of the manuscript, following these guidelines:

- *Figure.*   Three lines below the running head, insert the figure in the highest quality possible, with sharp contrast in photographs, distinct shading in bar graphs, and clear lettering in line graphs. Figures must be scaled to fit appropriately on the page.

- *Label.*   Below the figure, flush left, type the word *Figure*, the number of the figure, and a period. All of these elements are italicized.

- *Caption.*   One space after the figure label, type the caption, using sentence-style capitalization. Place a period at the end of the caption, even if it is not a complete sentence. The caption is *not* italicized.

- *Spacing and indentation.*   Figure captions are double-spaced. If a caption extends beyond one line, it continues flush left.

- *Fonts.*   Printed text that is part of a figure—labels, for example—should use a sans serif font such as Helvetica. The minimum acceptable font size is 8 points, with 14 points being the maximum.

- *Paging.*   Each figure must be presented on a separate page.

Special Concerns for Figures

- *Value of the figure.*   Consider whether the figure presents information more effectively than would a textual discussion or a table. Because figures are more difficult to prepare than print-based elements, make sure that your time is well spent in creating one.

Special Concerns for Figures

- *Computer-generated figures.* Today's word-processing programs are capable of creating a wide range of figures, including bar graphs, line graphs, and pie charts. Allow sufficient time to familiarize yourself with the procedures for creating a figure.

- *Visual clutter.* Include only figures that highlight important elements of your discussion. To achieve this goal, eliminate all extraneous detail in graphs, charts, and drawings and crop (trim) photographs and maps to focus visual attention on key features, not superficial or unrelated elements.

- *Visual clarity.* To ensure that figures achieve maximum impact, make sure that the print quality of graphs and charts is high (best achieved by laser printing). Furthermore, make sure that bar charts, photographs, and maps are sharply focused and have clear tonal contrast.

APPENDICES

One or more appendices can follow figures and continue the page numbering of the entire manuscript. Each appendix should adhere to the following guidelines:

- *Heading.* Three lines below the running head, type the word *Appendix*, centered but not italicized. If more than one appendix is included, label each one with a letter (Appendix A, Appendix B).

- *Appendix title.* Two lines below the heading, type the title of the appendix, centered, with headline-style capitalization.

- *Text.* Begin the text two lines below the appendix title; appended material is double-spaced.

- *Paging.* Each appendix begins on a new page.

2b General Manuscript Guidelines

In preparing a paper in APA style, writers must conform to a variety of principles, each of which is described in the following sections.

PAPER

Use heavy-weight, white bond, 8½" × 11" paper. Avoid light-weight paper because it does not hold up well under review or grading.

FONT SELECTION

Fonts—designed versions of letters, numbers, and characters—appear in different sizes, referred to as *points*. APA encourages the use of serif fonts (those with cross marks on individual letters) for the text of the paper; Times New Roman is the preferred font. Sans serif fonts (those without cross marks) such as Helvetica or Century Gothic may be used to label figures and illustrations. Font sizes for all elements of the paper except figures should be 12 points, the default size in most word-processing programs. (*NOTE:* Within figures, APA allows fonts from 8 to 14 points.)

Use italics (*slanted type*), not underlining, in all parts of your paper. Use your word-processing program's capabilities to insert accents, diacritical marks, and symbols directly in your paper, rather than adding them by hand.

LINE SPACING

Double-space all parts of the paper except elements within tables and figures, which use single-spacing. For visual clarity, you may triple- or quadruple-space before or after equations or other visual elements. (*NOTE:* Three lines separate the running head from the elements of the paper.)

WORD SPACING

Use two spaces after periods, question marks, and exclamation points (end punctuation). Use one space after commas, colons, and semicolons (internal punctuation); periods with initials (E. V. Debbs); and between elements in citations. No space is required with periods in abbreviations (p.m., e.g., U.S.), with hyphens (first-year student), or with dashes (example: The sounds of vowels—*a, e, i, o, u*—must be transcribed carefully to record speech accurately).

MARGINS AND INDENTATIONS

Leave 1-inch margins at the left, right, top, and bottom of each page. If the "default" margins for your word-processing program are not 1 inch, reset them to 1 inch. Do not justify the right margin (that is, create a straight text edge on the right); instead, use left justification, which aligns the text on the left but leaves the right margin irregular (ragged). Do not hyphenate words at the ends of lines.

A five- to seven-space indentation (½ inch)—best achieved by using the "Tab" feature—is required at the beginning of paragraphs and for the first line of footnotes. The continuous indentation that is required for long quotations and for second and subsequent lines of reference-list entries is best achieved by using the "Indent" feature.

SERIATION

To indicate a series or a sequence within a prose paragraph, enclose lowercase letters in parentheses. Although this pattern should not be overused, it has two advantages: (a) it provides visual clarity, and (b) it makes a long sentence with multiple elements easily readable. To achieve a similar effect with a series of set-off sentences or paragraphs, use Arabic numerals followed by periods:

1. Indent the number five to seven spaces from the margin (½ inch).

2. After a period and one space, type the sentence or paragraph.

3. If the item continues beyond one line, subsequent lines can be flush left or indented.

When elements are not presented in chronological order or by order of importance, they may be set off using bullets (typically filled circles or squares):

- This pattern draws attention to each element.

- The order of elements is deemphasized.

- Indentation patterns are the same as for numbered lists.

PAGING (RUNNING HEAD)

On the first line of the title page, flush left, type the words *Running head* (not italicized, but followed by a colon) and an abbreviated version of the paper's title. The title is typed in all capital letters and can contain no more than 50 characters (letters, numbers, symbols, punctuation, and spaces). Flush right, insert the page number. This information must be at least one-half inch from the top of the page; the text begins three lines below the running head (see pages 117 and 127 for samples). On subsequent pages of the paper, use only the running head itself, omitting the label "Running head" (see pages 118 and 128 for samples).

Use the "Header" feature of your word-processing program to type the running head and use codes to insert page numbers automatically throughout the document.

HEADINGS FOR SECTIONS

Use headings to divide and subdivide the paper into logical, and sometimes sequential, sections. APA establishes five potential levels of division for manuscripts, while acknowledging that most writing does not require the use of all five:

- *Level-1 headings*   are centered, with headline-style capitalization and boldface type.
- *Level-2 headings*   are flush left, with headline-style capitalization and boldface type.
- *Level-3 headings*   are indented, with sentence-style capitalization, boldface type, and a period.
- *Level-4 headings*   are indented, with sentence-style capitalization, boldface italic type, and a period.
- *Level-5 headings*   are indented, with sentence-style capitalization, italic type, and a period.

One level of division

Level-1 Heading

Two levels of division

Level-1 Heading

Level-2 Heading

Three levels of division

Level-1 Heading

Level-2 Heading

   Level-3 heading.

Four levels of division

> Level-1 Heading
> **Level-2 Heading**
>> Level-3 Heading.
>>> *Level-4 heading.*

Five levels of division

> Level-1 Heading
> **Level-2 Heading**
>> Level-3 Heading.
>>> *Level-4 heading.*
>>>> *Level-5 heading.*

When new headings are required, do not begin new pages. Simply type the new heading two lines below the last line of the preceding paragraph.

SUBMITTING THE PAPER

Submit manuscripts according to your instructor's guidelines, acknowledging that alternative formats exist:

- *Paper:*   Secure the pages with a paper clip in the upper-left corner and place them in a manila envelope with your name and affiliation typed or written on the outside. Always keep a photocopy—or another printed copy—of the paper.
- *Disk:*   Submit a copy of the final paper on a separate disk, clearly labeled with your name and affiliation, as well as a note about the word-processing program you used. Save a copy of the file on another disk for yourself.
- *Electronic:*   Attach the file version of the paper to an e-mail with a clear subject line (Paper 4: Test Anxiety), as well as a note about the word-processing program you used. If you do not receive confirmation of delivery, resubmit the e-mail and attachment. Print a copy of your e-mail as a record.

3   Following APA Editorial Style

Generally, APA style follows conventions that need little explanation (for example, periods follow sentences that make statements, and question marks follow sentences that pose questions). However, in some situations, agreement about editorial issues is not universal. (Should commas separate *all* elements of listed items? Are prepositions in titles capitalized?) In such special circumstances, follow the APA guidelines in this chapter to ensure that your manuscript meets expectations.

3a   Punctuation and Mechanics

PERIODS

Periods most often serve as end punctuation (after sentences), but they are also used with abbreviations and in other specialized contexts.

Uses of periods	Examples
End of a complete sentence	Periods end most sentences.
Initials with an author's name	C. S. Lewis
Reference-list abbreviations	Ed., Vol. 6, pp. 34–38, Rev. ed.
After figure captions	*Figure 3.* Student use of computers.
Latin abbreviations	i.e., e.g., vs., p.m.
U.S. when used as an adjective	U.S. government, U.S. economy
Abbreviation for inch	in. (distinct from the preposition *in*)
Decimal points in fractions	2.45 ml, 33.5 lb

COMMAS

Commas are internal forms of punctuation, most often used to separate elements within sentences. However, they also serve a few other purposes.

Uses of commas	*Examples*
Three or more items in a series	men, women, and children
Set off nonessential information	The room, which was well lighted, was on the south corridor.
Clauses of a compound sentence	The first survey was a failure, but the second one was a success.
Years with exact dates	May 25, 2010, the experiment began. *But* May 2010, the experiment began.
Years within in-text citations	(Armstrong, 2009); (Romines, 2010)
Numbers of 1,000 or larger	11,205 students, 1,934 books [see "Number Style," pages 51–52, for exceptions]

SEMICOLONS

In APA style, semicolons serve two purposes, one related to compound sentences and one related to elements in a series.

Uses of semicolons	*Examples*
Join clauses of a compound sentence when no coordinating conjunction is used	Males responded positively; females responded negatively.
Separate elements in a series when the elements contain commas	The test groups were from Fresno, California; St. Louis, Missouri; and Raleigh, North Carolina.

COLONS

Colons serve five distinct purposes in APA style. A complete sentence must precede the colon, and if the explanatory material that follows a colon is a complete sentence, the first word is capitalized.

Uses of colons	*Examples*
Introduce a phrase that serves as an explanation or illustration	Two words triggered the strongest reactions: *preferential* and *special*.
Introduce a sentence that serves as an explanation or illustration (the first word of the clarifying sentence is capitalized)	The results are quickly summarized: The experiment was a failure.
Separate elements in a ratio	The ratio was 3:10.
Separate the place of publication and publisher in a reference list entry	Didion, J. (2005). *The year of magical thinking.* New York, NY: Vintage Books.
Separate the numbered section and page number in a reference-list entry for a newspaper	Page, C. (2010, April 16). One very big thumbs down. *The Chicago Tribune*, p. 1:19.

DASHES

Formed by typing two hyphens (with no spaces before and after) or using the em-dash feature of your word-processing program, dashes serve a few selected purposes; however, they should be used sparingly in academic writing. Also note that if a title contains a dash, the word that follows the dash is capitalized.

Uses of dashes	*Examples*
Indicate a break in the thought of the sentence	The national heritage of participants—they identified themselves—proved less important than researchers anticipated.
Insert a series of elements that contain commas	Universities in two small cities—Terre Haute, Indiana, and Bloomington, Illinois—offer similar programs in psychology.

The shorter and more specialized en dash, which can be inserted using your word-processing program, is used to indicate inclusive pages in reference-list entries and in-text citations (102–133, pp. 435–436) and to show equal weight in a compound modifier (parent–teacher conference, doctor–patient relationship).

HYPHENS

Hyphens are most often used to join compound words that precede the noun they modify; this pattern ensures that modification is clear in individual sentences (example: First-person narratives are seldom suitable in academic writing). When the modifiers follow the noun, they are generally written without hyphens (example: The opening paragraphs were written in the first person). When general usage determines that a compound has become a permanent part of the language, it may be spelled either open (high school) or closed (casebook); consult a collegiate dictionary for individual cases.

Uses of hyphens	*Examples*
A compound that functions as an adjective	high-risk behaviors, time-intensive work, all-or-nothing approach
A compound with a number that functions as an adjective	two-part explanation, sixth-grade teacher, 50-word paragraph
A compound using the prefix *self-*	self-help books, self-inflicted injuries, self-imposed limitations
A compound that could be misread	re-form ("form again," not "change"), re-mark ("mark again," not "comment"), re-count ("count again," not "remember")
A compound using a prefix when the base word is capitalized	anti-American sentiment, pseudo-Freudian interpretation, post-Depression regulations
A compound using a prefix when the base word is a number	pre-1960s complacency, post-2009 requirements

Uses of hyphens	*Examples*
A compound using a prefix when the base word is more than one word	non-user-friendly instructions, anti-off-site testing, non-peer-reviewed journals
A fraction used as an adjective	three-fourths majority
A prefix that ends with the first letter of the base word (except *e*)	anti-inflammatory drug, post-traumatic stress (but preexisting condition)

Special cases—No hyphenation	*Examples*
A compound with an adverb ending in *-ly*	newly designed test, recently certified teacher, uncharacteristically exaggerated statement
A compound with a comparative or superlative adjective	less capable practitioner, clearer written instructions, most egregious error
A foreign phrase used as a modifier	ad hoc committee, a priori reasoning, laissez faire attitude
A common fraction used as a noun	two thirds of students, one half of the sample, one quarter of the residents

QUOTATION MARKS

Quotation marks are used within the text of a paper to identify titles of brief works, to indicate a quotation containing fewer than 40 words, and to highlight words used in special ways. *NOTE:* Quotation marks are not used in reference-list entries, and quotations of more than 40 words are indented and use no quotation marks. (See section 4f for additional information on quoted material.)

Uses of quotation marks	*Examples*
Titles of chapters, articles, songs, subsites of websites, and so on (quotation marks are used in the text only; reference-list entries *do not* use quotation marks)	"The High-Risk Child" (chapter), "Grant Writing vs. Grant Getting" (article), "My Vietnam" (song), "Adlerian Web Links" (subsite)
Quoted material (written or spoken) of fewer than 40 words when used word for word	Duncan (2010) asserted, "Normative behavior is difficult to define because community standards apply" (p. 233).
Words used counter to their intended meaning (irony, slang, or coined usage)	Her "abnormal" behavior was, in fact, quite normal.

PARENTHESES

Parentheses are used, always in pairs, to separate information and elements from the rest of the sentence.

Uses of parentheses	*Examples*
Set off clarifying information	We provided parents with four samples (see Figures 1–4).
Set off publication dates in in-text summaries.	Wagner (2009) noted that special-needs students responded well to the protocol.
Set off parenthetical references within the text; they must correspond to entries in the reference list.	First-time offenders are more likely to respond to group therapy sessions than are repeat offenders (Gillum & Sparks, 2010).
Set off page references that follow direct quotations	Sanchez (2009) noted, "Self-concept is an intangible quality among immigrant children" (p. 34).

Uses of parentheses	Examples
Introduce an abbreviation to be used in place of a full name in subsequent sections of a paper	The American Psychological Association (APA) published its first guidelines for manuscript preparation in 1929. Since then, APA has updated its guidelines eight times.
Set off letters that indicate divisions or sequences within paragraphs	The test included sections on (a) vocabulary, (b) reading comprehension, and (c) inferences.

BRACKETS

Brackets are used within parentheses or quotation marks to provide clarifying information. Use brackets sparingly because they can become distracting in academic writing.

Uses of brackets	Examples
Clarifying information in a quotation	Thompson (2010) observed, "When [students] work in groups, they perform better" (p. 11). (Used to replace *they* in the original text.)
Parenthetical information already in parentheses	(See Figure 4 [Percentages of students with learning disabilities] for more details.)
Clarifying information in a reference-list entry	*Eternal sunshine of the spotless mind* [Motion picture].

SLASHES

Slashes serve very specialized functions, often related to the presentation of compounds, comparisons, and correlations.

Uses of slashes	*Examples*
Hyphenated compounds in alternatives	first-day/second-day experiences
Fractions (numerator/ denominator)	3/4, X + Y/Z
Represent *per* in units with a numerical value	0.7 ml/L
Indicate phonemes in English	/b/
Separate dual publication dates for reprinted works	Hirsch (1999/2009)

CAPITALIZATION

APA follows universally accepted patterns for most capitalization. However, APA uses two distinct capitalization patterns for titles—headline style and sentence style—depending on whether they appear in the text of the paper or in the reference list.

Uses of capitalization	*Examples*
Proper nouns and proper adjectives	Jean Piaget, Robert Coles, Chinese students, Elizabethan drama
Specific departments (and academic units) in universities and specific courses	Department of Psychology, Indiana State University, Criminology 235
Trade and brand names	Prozac, Xerox, WordPerfect 12.0
Titles of articles or parts of books in the text: Use headline-style capitalization.	"The Middle-Child Syndrome," "Family Dynamics in a Changing World"
Nouns used with numbers or letters in describing sequenced methods or examples	Day 4, Experiment 6, Table 1, Figure 3
Formal titles of tests	Scholastic Aptitude Test
Table titles: Use headline-style capitalization.	*Grade Ranges of Remedial Students*

Uses of capitalization	*Examples*
First word of a sentence that follows a colon	One challenge could not be met: The cost of the test was too great.
Running head (all capitals)	BEYOND BIRTH ORDER, TEST QUESTIONS

Special cases—No capitalization	*Examples*
General references to departments and courses	a number of departments of sociology, a speech pathology course
Figure captions: Use sentence-style capitalization.	*Figure 1.* Percentages of international students by country of origin.
Generic or scientific names of drugs or ingredients	Fluoxetine hydrochloride (*but* Prozac)
Titles of articles or parts of books in in-text citations: Use sentence-style capitalization.	"The middle-child syndrome," "Family dynamics in a changing world"
General titles of tests	an achievement test

Capitalization of Titles

APA follows two distinct patterns for the capitalization of titles: one within the text of a paper and one in the reference list and other supporting pages.

- *In-text capitalization.* In the text of a paper, both in your prose and in in-text citations (parenthetical notes), use headline-style capitalization, no matter what kind of source you use.

- *Reference-list (and other) capitalization.* In the reference list, only periodical titles use headline-style capitalization. The titles of articles and all other sources (such as books or broadcasts) use sentence-style capitalization.

- *Capitalization of special in-text elements.* Headline-style capitalization is used for titles of tables.

Article Title in the Text

Rothschild (2010), in "Partners in Treatment: Relational Psychoanalysis and Harm Reduction Therapy," described and analyzed two approaches to the treatment of at-risk patients, as well as advocated efforts to integrate their techniques.

Article Title in a Reference-List Entry

Rothschild, D. (2010). Partners in treatment: Relational psychoanalysis and harm reduction therapy. *Journal of Clinical Psychology, 66,* 136-149.

Book Title in the Text

In *The Mismeasure of Man,* Gould (1981) provided useful insights into the ethical and unethical uses to which intelligence tests can be put.

Book Title in a Reference-List Entry

Gould, S. J. (1981). *The mismeasure of man.* New York, NY: Norton.

NOTE: The running head of your written work appears in all capital letters.

Headline-Style Capitalization

Guiding principles
Capitalize the first and last word; capitalize all other words except articles, *to* (as part of an infinitive phrase), and conjunctions or prepositions of three or fewer letters.

Examples
Edwards's *Post-Operative Stress: A Guide for the Family,* "Agent of Change: The Educational Legacy of Thomas Dewey"

Sentence-Style Capitalization

Guiding principles
Capitalize the first word of a title or subtitle; otherwise, capitalize only proper nouns and proper adjectives.

Examples
Edwards's *Post-operative stress: A guide for the family,* "Agent of change: The educational legacy of Thomas Dewey"

ITALICS

APA requires the use of italics (slanted fonts, as in *this example*), rather than underlining, in computer-generated manuscripts.

Uses of italics	Examples
Titles of full-length works: periodicals, books, motion pictures, CDs, websites, and so on	*Journal of Cognitive Psychology* (journal), *Wordplay and Language Learning* (book), *A Beautiful Mind* (motion picture), *Back to Black* (CD), *The Victorian Web* (website)
Genus, species, or varieties	*Pan troglodytes verus* (common chimpanzee)
New terms (when introduced and defined; thereafter, presented without italics)	The term *Nisei*, meaning second-generation Japanese Americans
Words, letters, or phrases used as words, letters, or phrases	Different impressions are created by the words *small, diminutive, minute,* and *tiny.*
Words that could be misread	*more* specific detail (meaning additional detail that is specific)
Letters used as symbols or algebraic variables	$$IQ = \frac{MA \text{ (mental age)}}{CA \text{ (chronological age)}} \times 100$$
Titles of tables	*Factors That Influence School Choice*
Volume numbers for periodicals (in reference-list entries)	*American Journal of Nursing, 110; Developmental Psychology, 46*
Anchors for scales	Satisfaction ratings ranged from 1 (*very satisfied*) to 8 (*very dissatisfied*).

NUMBER STYLE

In APA style, numerals are used more frequently than words, whether in written texts or supporting materials; Arabic numerals are preferred in an APA-style text, rather than Roman numerals.

Uses of numerals	*Examples*
Numbers of 10 and larger	14 respondents, 26 chapters, 11th article
Numbers smaller than 10 when compared with numbers larger than 10	the 4th chapter of 20; 2 of 30 research subjects; 13 sources: 10 articles, 3 books
Numbers preceding units of measurement	6-in. mark, 300-mg capsule
Numbers used statistically or mathematically	7.5 of respondents, a ratio of 5:2, 9% of the sample, the 3rd percentile
Numbers that represent periods of time	6 years, 5 months, 1 week, 3 hours, 15 minutes, 7:15 p.m.
Numbers that represent dates	November 1, 2009; April 15, 2010
Numbers that represent ages	4-year-olds, students who are 8 years old
Numbers for population size	1 million citizens
Numbers that refer to participants or subjects	7 participants, 4 rhesus monkeys
Numbers that refer to points or scores on a scale	scores of 6.5 on an 8-point scale
Numbers for exact sums of money	A test costing $4.25, a $35 fee
Numbers used as numbers	a scale ranging from 1 to 5
Numbers that indicate placement in a series	Exam 4, Figure 9
Numbers for parts of books	Chapter 2, page 6
Numbers in a list of four or more numbers	The sample was composed of work groups with 2, 4, 6, and 8 members.
Numbers in the abstract for a paper	All numbers appear in numeral form.

Uses of words for numbers	Examples
Numbers smaller than 10 (see exceptions in the previous table)	two experimental models, three lists, one-topic discussion
Zero and one (when confusion is likely)	zero-percent increase, one-unit design
Numbers that begin sentences	Sixteen authors contributed to the collection. Thirteen people attended.
Numbers that begin titles	"Twelve Common Errors in Research," *Seven-Point Scales: Values and Limitations*
Numbers that begin headings	*Five Common Income Groups* (table heading)
Numbers in common fractions	two thirds of teachers, a reduction of three fourths
Numbers in common names and phrases	the Seven Deadly Sins, the Ten Commandments, the Seven Wonders of the World

Cardinal and Ordinal Numbers

Cardinal numbers (one, two, three, and so on) indicate quantity; ordinal numbers (first, second, third, and so on) indicate order. The principles described in the preceding tables apply whether the numbers are cardinal or ordinal.

Commas in Numbers

In most writing contexts, commas are used in numbers of 1,000 or larger. Place commas between groups of three digits, moving from the right. However, in the following situations, commas are not used.

Numbers without commas	Examples
Page numbers	page 1287, pages 1002–1021, (p. 2349)
Degrees of temperature	2044°F

(cont. on next page)

Numbers without commas	*Examples*
Serial numbers	033776901
Binary digits	01100100
Numbers to the right of decimal points	2.09986
Designations of acoustical frequency	1000 Hz
Degrees of freedom	$F(31, 1000)$

Plurals of Numbers

Whether numbers are presented as numerals or words, form their plurals by adding only *s* or *es:* 1960s, threes, sixes, 25s. Do not use apostrophes to indicate plurality.

Numbered Seriation

To indicate series, sequences, or alternatives in a series of set-off sentences or paragraphs, use Arabic numerals, followed by periods (see page 35).

3b   General Style

The way in which a manuscript is written affects the ways in which readers respond. A well-written paper communicates ideas efficiently and effectively, whereas a poorly written paper distracts readers from its central ideas. Therefore, take time to revise your writing to improve its presentation, paying special attention to elements that improve the effectiveness of communication.

TRANSITIONS

Transitions—words or phrases that signal relationships among elements of your writing—facilitate readers' progress through a paper. Use transitional words and phrases to create appropriate links within your work.

Transitional Words and Phrases

Relationship	*Examples*
Addition	also, and, besides, equally, further, furthermore, in addition, moreover, next, too

Relationship	*Examples*
Similarity	also, likewise, moreover, similarly
Difference	but, however, in contrast, nevertheless, on the contrary, on the other hand, yet
Examples	for example, for instance, in fact, specifically, to illustrate
Restatements	finally, in brief, in conclusion, in other words, in short, in summary, on the whole, that is, therefore, to sum up
Results	accordingly, as a result, consequently, for this reason, so, therefore, thereupon, thus
Chronology	after, afterward, before, during, earlier, finally, first, immediately, in the meantime, later, meanwhile, next, second, simultaneously, soon, still, then, third, when, while
Location	above, below, beyond, farther, here, nearby, opposite, there, to the left, to the right, under

VERB TENSE

Verbs are primary communicators in sentences, signaling action *(organized, summarized, presented)* or indicating a state of being *(seemed, was)*. Well-chosen, specific verbs make writing direct and forceful. Moreover, tenses of verbs indicate chronology, clarifying the time relationships that you want to express.

In APA style, verbs are used in specific ways to signal ideas clearly.

Uses of verbs	*Examples*
Active voice (to clarify who is doing what)	Respondents completed the questionnaire in 15 minutes. (*Not*: The questionnaire was completed in 15 minutes by the respondents.) *(cont. on next page)*

Uses of verbs	Examples
Passive voice (to clarify who or what received the action, not the person or people responsible)	Traditional IQ tests were administered as part of the admissions process. (The use of the tests is emphasized, not the givers of the tests.)
Past tense (to place an action in the past or to describe previous research)	Bradshaw and Hines (2005) summarized their results in one incisive paragraph.
Present perfect tense (to describe an action that began in the past and continues to the present or to describe a concept with continued application)	In the years since, researchers have incorporated Piaget's methods in a variety of studies of children.
Subjunctive mood (to describe a conditional situation or one contrary to fact)	If the sampling were larger, the results might be different.

AGREEMENT

Agreement is the matching of words or word forms according to number (singular and plural) and gender (masculine, feminine, or neuter). Verbs take singular or plural forms depending on whether their subjects are singular or plural.

Subject–Verb Agreement

Special circumstances	Examples
Foreign words—*datum* (singular) versus *data* (plural), *phenomenon* (singular) versus *phenomena* (plural), and others: Choose the correct form.	The data suggest that our preconceptions were ill founded. (plural subject/plural verb) The phenomenon is unlikely to occur again. (singular subject/singular verb)

Special circumstances	Examples
Collective (or group) nouns: Consider whether members of the group act in unison (singular) or individually (plural).	The couple initiates the counseling sessions. (singular meaning to stress shared action) The couple meet separately with the counselor. (plural meaning to stress individual action)
Singular and plural subjects joined by *or* or *nor*: Match the verb to the nearer subject.	Neither the parents nor the therapist finds their meetings helpful. Or: Neither the therapist nor the parents find their meetings helpful.

Pronouns must match their antecedents (the words to which they refer) in both number and gender.

Pronoun–Antecedent Agreement

Common circumstances	Examples
Agreement in number: Match the pronoun to its antecedent. (*Also see* "Biased Language," pages 58–60.)	A participant secures his or her stipend from the controller's office. (singular) Participants secure their stipends from the controller's office. (plural)
Agreement in gender: Match the pronoun to the antecedent. (*Also see* "Biased Language.")	Devon was the first student to complete his booklet. (masculine) The lab rat (subject 3) stopped eating its food during the experiment. (neuter)
Who and *whom*: Use *who* in a subject position; use *whom* in an object position.	Who is responsible for compiling the data? (subject: *He* or *she* is.) To whom should we address our inquiries? (object: Address them to *him* or *her*.)

PARALLELISM

Parallelism is the use of equivalent forms when words are used together: nouns, verbs of the same tense or form, and so on.

Parallels	Examples
Elements in a series: Use matching forms.	Even young children are expected to add, to subtract, and to multiply. (parallel verb forms) Reading, writing, speaking, listening, and thinking compose the language arts. (parallel gerund/ noun forms)
Correlative conjunctions (*both/and, either/or, neither/nor, not only/ but also*): Use matching forms of the words, phrases, and clauses that are linked.	The youngest child in a large family is either the most independent or the least independent of the siblings. (parallel phrases) We found not only that the experiment was too costly but also that it was too time consuming. (parallel clauses)

3c Word Choice

Word choice makes meaning clear to readers. Specific word choices affect the tone of writing—implying your perception of yourself, your readers, your subject, and your purpose in writing. Consequently, choose words carefully to communicate ideas effectively.

NOUN CLUSTERS

Noun clusters are created when nouns, often in multiples, are used to modify yet another noun. Although the modification patterns may be grammatically correct (nouns *can* function as modifiers), they often create dense clusters of meaning that have to be sorted through carefully.

For example, the phrase *freshman student success ensurance initiative* is overly long, does not read smoothly, and has to be deconstructed. To improve readability, untangle the nouns and place them in easily readable phrases: *an initiative to ensure the success of freshman students.* The reconstructed phrase is easier to interpret than the original and, therefore, communicates the idea more efficiently than does the original.

JARGON

Jargon is the specialized language of a professional group. In some instances, a specific technical term communicates an idea more efficiently than an explanation in everyday language. For instance, the phrase *correlational analyses* explains in two generally understood words a process by which data are both systematically linked and logically compared. However, in many instances, common language that is well selected communicates ideas in a more straightforward and less pretentious way than jargon does. For example, in many instances the phrase *classroom teacher* communicates an idea with greater clarity and less distraction than the more affected phrase *teacher/practitioner,* which is a stilted way of expressing an idea that is implicit in the word *teacher.*

In your writing, choose words with care. Use technical jargon only when it communicates ideas clearly and efficiently—that is, when it is precise and helpful. Never use jargon to impress, because an over-reliance on technical terms (especially those that do not communicate ideas precisely and quickly) frustrates readers and clutters prose.

COLLOQUIALISMS

In academic writing, avoid colloquialisms—expressions that are better suited for conversation and other forms of informal communication. Words and phrases such as *write-up* (instead of *report*), *only a few* (rather than *7%*), or *get-together* (in place of *meeting* or *colloquium*) not only lack the specificity of more technical, formal language but also suggest a lack of precision that may make readers question the care with which you have described your research. For these reasons, use precise, professional language in your writing.

SPECIFICITY

Choose specific words to create clear meaning; do not assume that readers will infer meaning from vague language. For example, rather than writing that a survey contained *numerous questions,* be specific and indicate that it contained

75 questions. Instead of noting that a study was based on the responses of *many Midwestern students,* describe the research group more precisely: *4,000 freshman students in Indiana, Illinois, Missouri, and Iowa.* Even this description could be made more specific by noting the percentage of male/female respondents, the kinds of schools (liberal arts colleges, small state universities, large state universities, and so on), and the locations of the schools (urban, rural, and so on).

The credibility of research depends on using language that communicates clearly. Consequently, choose words that are as specific as possible.

BIASED LANGUAGE

Whether employed consciously or unconsciously, the use of biased language conveys a writer's insensitivity, ignorance, or, in some instances, prejudice—any of which disrupts communication because readers expect to find balance and fairness in what they read. Writing that incorporates biased language reflects badly on the writer, alienates thoughtful readers, and consequently interferes with effective communication.

As a writer, you should make a conscious effort to use accurate, equitable language. Recognizing that your potential readers represent a broad spectrum of society, choose words with care and avoid stereotypes.

Racial and Ethnic Bias

Language that is racially and ethnically biased often relies on dated words related to racial or ethnic groups. In other instances, racially and ethnically biased word choices ignore the distinct groups that exist within larger classifications, thereby perpetuating broad stereotypes. Consequently, it is preferable to refer to racial or ethnic groups as specifically as possible.

Preferred Racial or Ethnic Terms		
Questionable	*Preferred terms for American citizens*	*Preferred terms for non-American citizens*
Arab	Arab American; *or* Saudi American, Iraqi American, and so on	Saudi, Iraqi, Afghan, and so on

Questionable	Preferred terms for American citizens	Preferred terms for non-American citizens
Hispanic	Latino/Latina, Chicano/Chicana; *or* Cuban American, and so on	Mexican, Cuban, Costa Rican, and so on
Indian	Native American; *or* Cherokee, Ogallala Sioux, Seminole, and so on	Mesoamerican, Inuit, and so on
Black	African American; *or* Kenyan American, and so on	African; *or* Ugandan, Kenyan, and so on
White	European American; *or* Italian American, French American, Irish American, and so on	Caucasian, European; *or* German, French, Hungarian, Russian, and so on
Oriental	Asian American; *or* Japanese American, Korean American, Chinese American, and so on	Asian; *or* Korean, Japanese, Vietnamese, and so on

Gender Bias

Language based on stereotypical gender roles—also called *sexist language*—implies through choices of nouns, pronouns, and adjectives that people fall into preassigned roles. Because gender-biased language fails to reflect the diversity of contemporary society, it is inaccurate. Replace nouns that imply gender exclusivity—for example, *chairman* or *spokesman*—with words whose gender meanings are neutral *(chairperson* or *spokesperson)*.

Avoid using gender-specific pronouns when their antecedents are not gender specific. The most common concern is the generic use of a masculine pronoun *(he, him, his, himself)*, as in this sentence: "A psychiatrist is bound by professional oath to keep his patients' records confidential." Although this usage was once acceptable, today's writers and readers expect pronoun use to be inclusive, not exclusionary. Solutions include using alternative pronouns ("A psychiatrist is bound by professional oath to keep his or her patients' records confidential."), plural forms ("Psychiatrists are bound by professional oath to keep their patients' records confidential."), and omission of the pronoun when no confusion is likely ("A psychiatrist is bound by professional oath to keep patients' records confidential.").

Avoid using gender-related adjectives when other modifiers create similar meaning without bias or when gender is not an issue. "The male nurse was both competent and friendly, reassuring the patient and family members" is better presented this way: "The nurse was both competent and friendly, reassuring the patient and family members."

Other Forms of Bias

Be sensitive to the ways in which your language characterizes people by age, class, religion, region, physical and mental ability, or sexual orientation. Do your word choices create stereotypical impressions that disrupt your discussions? Do they convey unintended but negative feelings? Will they offend potential readers and therefore distract them from your ideas? Examine your writing carefully for instances of these kinds of bias and explore alternative ways to convey your meaning.

Biased Language in a Historical Context

Historical texts often contain language that violates today's standards of usage. However, if you quote from such a text, you should retain the original language. The date in the in-text reference will allow readers to place the language in the correct historical context. If the language is particularly troublesome, you may insert an asterisk (*) following the first use of the word or phrase and provide commentary in a footnote.

4 Preparing the Reference List and In-Text Citations

The reference list provides comprehensive information on each of the sources used in a paper. By listing the author (or authors) of each source—along with publication dates, full titles, and information about publishers (producers, distributors, or websites)—writers ensure that readers can locate sources for further study.

Sources that appear in the reference list must be cited in the paper using parallel information. For example, if a reference-list entry includes two authors, then the in-text citation must also include both authors' names (see "In-Text Citations" later in this chapter). For this reason, writers should prepare reference-list entries for sources before writing the paper.

This chapter includes detailed discussions of the information required for a reference list, as well as its formatting requirements; Chapters 5 to 8 provide explanations and examples of the most commonly used sources for APA papers. In addition, this book provides information on some sources that are not traditionally used in APA journal articles (the writing done by professionals) but that are potentially useful for students' writing; the principles of APA documentation style have been applied in preparing these sample entries.

4a The Reference List—An Overview

A reference list is an alphabetically arranged list of sources used in a paper. It starts on a new page immediately after the last text page of the paper, continues the page numbering, and is also double-spaced. It is introduced by the word *References* (centered but not italicized); if the reference list continues on a second page, no additional heading is required. Entries in the reference list follow the formats described in this chapter. (See pages 125 and 134 for the reference lists of the sample papers.)

4b Information for APA Entries

Entries for the reference list vary because of the different information they include. All, however, must follow an established order for presenting information:

1. *Authors (and editors).* Take names from the first page of an article or from the title page of a book.

Authors' or editors' names are listed in the order in which they appear (not alphabetical order), and initials are used instead of first or middle names. *All* authors' names are inverted (last name first), not just the name of the first author. The names of group, institutional, or organizational authors are spelled out completely. If a book has eight or more authors, the first six are listed, followed by ellipsis points (three spaced periods) and the name of the last author.

2. *Publication dates.* For professional journals and books, include the publication year in parentheses. For sources that use specific dates—such as popular magazines, newspapers, television broadcasts, or websites—include the year and the month or the year, month, and day in parentheses. When a source has no author, the entry begins with the title, followed by the date.

3. *Titles.* List titles completely, taking information from the first page of an article or from the title page of a book. Include both titles and subtitles, no matter how long they are.

4. *Additional information.* Include any of the following information in the order presented here if it is listed on the first page of the article, essay, chapter or other subsection, or the title page of the book:

   • Translator
   • Edition number
   • Volume number
   • Issue number (if the journal is paginated separately by issue)
   • Inclusive pages

5. *Facts of publication.* For periodicals, take the volume number, issue number (if needed), and date from the first few pages in journals and magazines, often in combination with the table of contents, or from the masthead (a listing of information at the top of the first page of newspapers). For books, use the first city listed on the title page and provide a two-letter abbreviation for the state or the full name of the foreign country. Take the publisher's name from the title page, presenting it in abbreviated form (see the following box for

explanations of how to shorten publishers' names and Chapters 5 to 8 for samples within entries). Use the most recent date from the copyright page (which immediately follows the title page).

6. *Retrieval information.* For electronic sources, provide a retrieval statement, a phrase or sentence that explains how to access the source, to direct readers to the electronic copy.

Shortened Forms of Publishers' Names

Use the full names of associations and corporations that serve as publishers.	American Psychological Association, National Council of Teachers of English (These publishers' names appear in their full forms.)
Use the full names of university presses.	Harvard University Press, University of Illinois Press (These publishers' names appear in their full forms.)
Use full names for government publishers.	U.S. Government Printing Office (This name appears in its full form.)
Drop given names or initials.	Harry N. Abrams is shortened to Abrams.
Use the first of multiple names.	Farrar, Straus, and Giroux is shortened to Farrar.
Drop corporation designations: *Publishers, Company, Incorporated,* and so on.	Doubleday and Co., Inc. is shortened to Doubleday.
Retain the words *Books* and *Press*.	Bantam Books, American Psychiatric Press (These publishers' names appear in their full forms.)

4c   Format for APA Entries

To ensure easy reading, entries for the reference list must follow this format:

- *Indentation patterns.*   Begin the first line of each entry at the left margin; indent subsequent lines five to seven spaces (½ inch), using the "Indent" feature.

- *Authors' names.* Because entries must be arranged in alphabetical order, invert all authors' names (Haley, R.) and use an ampersand (&), not the word *and,* to join the names of multiple authors (Haley, R., & Taylor, J.).

- *Authorless sources.* When no author is identified, list the source by title. Alphabetize a reference-list entry by using the primary words of the title (excluding *a, an,* or *the*). When an authorless book has an editor, you can, as an alternative, begin the entry with his or her name.

- *Article titles.* Include full titles but use sentence-style capitalization. Article titles use no special punctuation in a reference-list entry (although they are placed in quotation marks and use headline-style capitalization in in-text citations and in the paper).

- *Periodical titles.* Present the titles of periodicals in headline style (all major words capitalized). Follow the title with a comma and the volume number. Italicize the title *and* the volume number, including the separating comma and the comma that follows the volume number.

- *Issue numbers.* If a journal paginates issues separately, place the issue number in parentheses after the volume number; no space separates the volume number from the issue number, and the parentheses and issue number are *not* italicized. Both volume and issue numbers are presented as Arabic, not Roman, numerals.

- *Titles of books.* Present the titles of books with sentence-style capitalization. The title is italicized. (Headline-style capitalization is used in the paper.)

- *Publishers' names.* Shorten the names of commercial publishers to a brief but clear form, using only the main elements of their names (*Houghton,* not *Houghton Mifflin*) and dropping descriptive titles (*Publishers, Company, Incorporated*). However, use the complete names of university presses and organizations and corporations that serve as publishers, retaining the words *Books* and *Press* whenever they are part of a publisher's name. If a work has co-publishers, include both publishers' names, separated by an en dash or a hyphen (Harvard–Belknap Press).

- *Punctuation within entries.* Separate major sections of entries (author, date, title, and publication information) with periods, including elements enclosed in parentheses or brackets; the period used with the abbreviation of an author's first or middle name substitutes for this period.

However, separate the place of publication from the publisher's name with a colon. When an entry ends with a DOI or URL, no period is required to close the entry.

- *Spacing within entries.*   One space separates elements in APA entries. However, when a journal paginates issues separately, the issue number (in parentheses) follows the volume number without a space.

- *Abbreviations.*   Use abbreviations for standard parts of periodicals, books, and other print materials. (See the following box for a list of acceptable abbreviations.)

- *Page numbers.*   When citing articles in periodicals or chapters or other portions of complete works, list page numbers completely (*176–179,* not *176–9* or *176–79*), separated by an en dash or a hyphen. Journals and magazines list page numbers without page abbreviations; however, page references for newspapers, books, and other print materials use the abbreviations *p.* (for *page*) and *pp.* (for *pages*). No commas are used to separate digits of numbers one thousand or larger when citing pages (*pp. 1295–1298*). When articles appear on nonconsecutive pages, list them all, separated by commas (*34–35, 38, 54–55, 57, 59*).

- *Line spacing.*   The entire reference list is double-spaced.

Acceptable Abbreviations

Digital Object Identifier	DOI or doi
edition	ed.
Editor (Editors)	Ed. (Eds.)
no date	n.d.
No place of publication	N.p.
no publisher	n.p.
Number	No.
page (pages)	p. (pp.)
Part	Pt.
Revised edition	Rev. ed.
Second edition, fifth edition	2nd ed., 5th ed. (superscript is not used)
Supplement	Suppl.
Technical Report	Tech. Rep.
Translator	Trans.
Uniform Resource Locator	URL
Volume (Volumes)	Vol. (Vols.)

4d   Alphabetizing the Reference List

The reference list must be in alphabetical order, which seems simple enough. Reality often proves more complicated, however, so use the guidelines in the following box.

Alphabetizing the Reference List

Circumstances	*Rule and sample*
Letter-by-letter style	Alphabetize one letter at a time: *Baker, R. L.* precedes *Baker, W. S.; Our American Heritage* comes before *Our American Legacy.*
"Nothing precedes something"	The space that follows a name supersedes the letters that follow: *Wood, T. S.,* precedes *Woodman, K. F.*
Prefixes	Prefixes are alphabetized as they appear, not as if they appeared in full form: *MacDonald, J. B.,* precedes *McDonald, B. V.*
Names with prepositions	Names that incorporate prepositions are alphabetized as if they were spelled closed: *De Forest, A. M.,* precedes *Denton, R. L.* (Consult a dictionary regarding patterns for names in different languages.)
Multiple works by the same author	Arrange selections in chronological order: *Sparks, C. G.* (2008) precedes *Sparks, C. G.* (2009)
Single-author and multiple-author works	Single-author works precede multiple-author works: *Kelly, M. J.,* precedes *Kelly, M. J.,* & *Dorfmeyer, P. G.*
Groups, institutions, or organizations as authors	Alphabetize group, institutional, or organizational authors by major words in their completely spelled-out names (omitting *a, an,* or *the*): *American Psychological Association* precedes *Anderson, V. W.*
Authorless works	Authorless works are alphabetized by the first significant words in their titles (omitting *a, an,* or *the*): *The price of poverty* precedes *Stewart, R. P.*
Numerals in titles	Numerals in titles are alphabetized as if they were spelled out: "The 10 common errors of research" precedes *Twelve angry men.*

4e　In-Text Citations

APA documentation has two areas of emphasis: (a) the authors of source materials and (b) the year in which sources were published or presented. This pattern is commonly described as the author–date style.

When incorporating information from a source, provide an in-text citation that includes, at minimum, the author's last name and the year of publication or presentation. The complexity of some sources may require the inclusion of additional information.

PATTERNS FOR IN-TEXT CITATIONS

An in-text citation (also called a parenthetical note) corresponds to an entry in the reference list at the end of the paper. The information in an entry for the reference list determines what information appears in a citation in the text. For example, if a reference-list entry for a source begins with the author's name, then the author's name appears in the in-text citation. If a reference-list citation for a source begins with the title, however, then the title (or a shortened version of it) appears in the in-text citation. If these correlations are clear and consistent, readers can turn from the paper's in-text citation to the reference list and readily locate the full entry for the source.

Shortened Forms of Titles

- *Use initial words of the title.*　Because readers will use the short title to find the full title in the reference list, use words at the beginning. "When Teachers Don't Make the Grade" can logically be shortened to "When Teachers."

- *Omit articles.*　*A, an,* and *the* should be dropped from the shortened title. *A Long Day's Journey into Night* can be shortened to *Long Day's Journey.*

- *Omit subtitles.*　Omit the clarifying information in the second part of a two-part title. "Paycare: The High Cost of Insurance-based Medicine" can be shortened to "Paycare."

- *Omit prepositional phrases.*　Omit prepositional phrases as the ends of titles. *The Price of Poverty* can be shortened to *Price.*

(cont. on next page)

Shortened Forms of Titles

- *Make the short title brief but readable.* Remember that the short title will be part of your text and should, consequently, read well. *The Chicago Manual of Style* shortens to *Chicago Manual; Chicago* alone might read awkwardly.

- *Retain punctuation patterns.* Follow the punctuation patterns required in the text: titles of articles, chapters, poems, and other brief works are placed in quotation marks; titles of journals, books, films, and other long works are italicized. Punctuate the shortened forms of titles as you would the complete forms. *APA Dictionary of Psychology* could be shortened to *APA Dictionary,* but it remains in italics.

BASIC FORMS OF IN-TEXT CITATIONS

To avoid disrupting the text, in-text citations identify only the last name of the author or a brief version of the title under which the source appears in the reference list, followed by the year of publication (even when reference-list entries require the month or month and day). For the sake of clarity and smoothness, you may incorporate some of the necessary information in your sentences. After the author and date have been introduced, the date may be omitted in subsequent references within the same paragraph.

> A variety of psychological and social factors influence the likelihood of smoking among adolescents: patterns of rebelliousness and impulsiveness, indications of low self-esteem or poor achievement, and modeled behavior among peers or family members (Young, 2005). Young also noted that attempts to ameliorate these behaviors were not always successful.

OR

> A variety of psychological and social factors influence the likelihood of smoking among adolescents. Young (2005) cited patterns of rebelliousness and impulsiveness, indications of low self-esteem or poor achievement, and modeled behavior among peers or family members. Young also noted that attempts to ameliorate these behaviors were not always successful.

Reference-list entry

Young, T. K. (2005). *Population health: Concepts and methods* (2nd ed.). New York, NY: Oxford University Press.

In special cases, the rule of using only the author's last name and the date is superseded:

Patterns for In-Text Citations

Special circumstances	*Rule and sample*
Two authors with the same last name	Include initials with the last name: (Barratt, J. D., 2009), distinct from (Barratt, L. K., 2010).
Multiple works by the same author (same year)	Use letters to distinguish the sources: (Morrison, 2010a), distinct from (Morrison, 2010b). The letters indicate the alphabetical order of the titles.
Multiple works by the same author (same note)	To cite several works by the same author (all included in the reference list), include the author's name and all dates in chronological order, separated by commas: (Vidich, 2007, 2008, 2010).
Three, four, or five authors	The first notation includes all names (Jarnow, Judelle, & Guerriro, 2009). *Subsequent* citations use the first author's name and *et al.*, not italicized: (Jarnow et al., 2009).
Six or more authors	Beginning with the first notation, use only the first author's name and *et al.*, not italicized: (Austen et al., 2010)
Two or more works by different authors (same note)	To cite several works by different authors in the same note, list each author (in alphabetical order) and date, separated by semicolons: (Bennet, 2008; Greene, 2007; Swift, 2009).

(cont. on next page)

Patterns for In-Text Citations

Organization as author	In the first note, present the organization's name in full, with an abbreviation in brackets: (National Council of Teachers of English [NCTE], 2010). Use the shortened form in subsequent citations: (NCTE, 2010).
No author	Include a shortened version of the title, appropriately capitalized and punctuated, and the year: ("Optimum Performance," 2008); (*Common Ground*, 2009). If "Anonymous" is the *explicit* attribution of a work, it is used in the author position: (Anonymous, 2010).
Multiple publication dates	Include both dates, separated by a slash: (Jagger & Richards, 1994/2001).
Reference works	List by author if applicable (Angermüller, 2009) or by a shortened form of the title ("Manhattan Project," 2009).
Parts of sources	When citing only a portion of a source—for example, a page to identify a quotation or a chapter in a general reference—include the author or title as appropriate, the date, and clarifying information: (Thomas, 2010, p. 451); (Spindrell, 2009, Chapters 2–3).
Personal communication (*NOTE*: Although cited in the text, personal communications do not have entries in the reference list. Initials are also used with the person's last name.)	Cite e-mail, correspondence, memos, interviews, and so on by listing the person's name, the clarifying phrase *personal communication* (not italicized), and the specific date (L. R. Bates, personal communication, March 7, 2010).

4f Quotations

When an author's manner of expression is unique or when his or her ideas or language are difficult to paraphrase or summarize, quote the passage in your text. To avoid plagiarism, reproduce quoted material word for word, including exact spelling and punctuation, separate the material from your text, and prepare an accurate citation.

The pattern for incorporating a quotation varies depending on its length. In-text citations for quotations also include specific page references.

Concerns About Quotations

Although quotations can enhance a paper by presenting the ideas of other writers in their own words, the overuse of quotations can become distracting. Therefore, assess the value of quotations by asking the following questions:

- *Style.* Is the style so distinctive that you cannot say the same thing as well or as clearly in your own words?

- *Vocabulary.* Is the vocabulary technical and therefore difficult to translate into your own words?

- *Reputation.* Is the author so well known or so important that the quotation can lend authority to your paper?

- *Points of contention.* Does the author's material raise doubts or questions or make points with which you disagree?

If you answer yes to any of these questions, then using the quotation is appropriate. If not, summarize the material instead.

BRIEF QUOTATIONS (FEWER THAN 40 WORDS)

A quotation of fewer than 40 words appears within a normal paragraph, with the author's words enclosed in quotation marks. The in-text citation, placed in parentheses, follows the closing quotation mark, whether it is in the middle or at the end of a sentence; if the quotation ends the sentence, the sentence's period follows the closing parenthesis. The citation includes the author's name and the publication date (unless they have been previously mentioned in the text), as well as a specific page reference, introduced with the abbreviation *p.* or *pp.* (not italicized). For example:

> The tacit assumption that intelligence is at the heart of success has been called into question: "The memory and analytical skills so central to intelligence are certainly important for school and life success, but perhaps they are not sufficient. Arguably, wisdom-related skills are at least as important or even more important" (Sternberg, 2003, p. 147).

OR

> The tacit assumption that intelligence is at the heart of success has been called into question. Sternberg (2003) observed: "The memory and analytical skills so central to intelligence are certainly important for school and life success, but perhaps they are not sufficient. Arguably, wisdom-related skills are at least as important or even more important" (p. 147).

Reference-list entry

Sternberg, R. J. (2003). *Wisdom, intelligence, and creativity synthesized.* Cambridge, England: Cambridge University Press.

LONG QUOTATIONS (40 OR MORE WORDS)

A quotation of 40 or more words is set off from a normal paragraph in an indented block paragraph. After an introductory statement, start the quotation on a new line, indented five to seven spaces or ½ inch (use the "Indent" feature to maintain the indentation throughout the quotation). Quotation marks do not appear at the opening and closing of a block quotation. Like the surrounding text, the quotation is double-spaced. Note that the period precedes the in-text citation with a block quotation. For example:

> Clements and Fiorentino (2004) articulated the value of children's play in their holistic development:
>> Play exists at the very heart of childhood. It is the fundamental means through which children learn about themselves, their family members, their local communities, and the world around them. The freedom to explore, experiment, make believe, and make one's choices is a key ingredient in the healthy development of every child. (p. xv)
>
> Current research in countries around the world reinforces this principle, even when the social and moral standards vary greatly from culture to culture.

Reference-list entry

Clements, R. L., & Fiorentino, L. H. (2004). [Introduction]. In
R. L. Clements & L. H. Fiorentino (Eds.), *The child's right
to play: A global approach* (pp. xv–xvi). Westport, CT:
Praeger.

PUNCTUATION WITH QUOTATIONS

Single Quotation Marks

To indicate an author's use of quotation marks within a
brief quotation (which is set off by double quotation marks),
change the source's punctuation to single quotation marks, as
in this example:

> Young (2005) stressed the cautionary and even alarmist
> nature of current approaches to health management. He
> asserted, "Each year as many as 40,000 to 50,000 articles
> are published where the term *risk* appears in the titles and
> abstracts—this has led some observers to refer to a 'risk
> epidemic' in the medical literature" (p. 177).

Reference-list entry

Young, T. K. (2005). *Population health: Concepts and methods*
(2nd ed.). New York, NY: Oxford University Press.

Because long block quotations do not begin and end with
quotation marks, the source's quotation marks remain double, as in this example:

> Borland (2003) posited:
>> Giftedness and gifted children are recent inventions
>> in education that can be traced to the advent of
>> psychometrics. It is no coincidence that the person
>> universally regarded as the "father" of gifted
>> education in this country, Lewis M. Terman, was
>> also the developer of the Stanford–Binet Intelligence
>> Scale. Individual differences in test scores, as well as
>> more apparent differences in academic achievement
>> as compulsory education laws became more
>> common and better enforced, can be seen as the
>> direct progenitor of such constructs as those
>> that later became giftedness and mental retardation.
>> (p. 107)
> Few scholars would question Terman's central role in
> assessing intelligence, but some would question the
> centrality of his role in the development of gifted programs.

Reference-list entry

Borland, J. H. (2003). The death of giftedness: Gifted education without gifted children. In J. H. Borland (Ed.), *Rethinking gifted education* (pp. 105–124). In *Education and Psychology of the Gifted Series*. New York, NY: Teachers College Press.

Brackets

Use brackets to indicate that you have either added words for clarity or introduced a substitution within a quotation. Most often, the words you add are specific nouns to substitute for pronouns that are vague outside the context of the original work. However, you may substitute a different tense of the same verb (for example, *used* for *use*). *NOTE:* A change in the capitalization at the beginning of a sentence, as well as a change in end punctuation to fit your syntax, does not require the use of brackets.

> In analyzing the problem-solving skills of creative people, Henderson (2004) observed:
>> [Inventors] recalled the freedom they were given to explore their surrounding environments and the tolerance their parents and educators showed if they made a mess, broke something, or shorted out electrical circuits as a result of their inventive endeavors. (p. 119)
>
> Such forbearance from adults, Henderson's study suggested, is integral to developing creative problem-solving skills.

Out of the context of her chapter, Henderson's original phrase—*The participants*—lacks specificity.

Reference-list entry

Henderson, S. J. (2004). Inventors: The ordinary genius next door. In R. J. Sternberg, E. L. Grigorenko, & J. L. Singer (Eds.), *Creativity: From potential to realization* (pp. 103–125). Washington, DC: American Psychological Association.

NOTE: Do not change dated language or material to make it more acceptable by today's standards; rather, let the material stand on its own and provide your own separate commentary. (See page 60.)

Ellipsis Points

Use ellipsis points—three spaced periods—to indicate where words have been omitted within a quotation. Ellipsis points are unnecessary at the beginning or end of a quotation, unless a quotation begins or ends in the middle of a sentence. To indicate an omission between sentences, retain the preceding sentence's punctuation (producing four spaced periods).

> Miller (2003) observed that socially constructed self-esteem is inextricably tied to other people's praise: "Flattery is narcotic and addicting. It preys on two desperate and inescapable desires: to be thought well of by others and to think well of ourselves. . . . They are complexly intertwined" (p. 96).
>
> [Omitted: "The second desire depends on the first more than the first on the second; in any event, . . ."]

Reference-list entry

Miller, W. I. (2003). *Faking it.* Cambridge, England: Cambridge University Press.

5 Citing Periodicals

Most often affiliated with professional organizations, journals are scholarly publications whose articles are subjected to careful review. Often called refereed journals, they are the mainstay of much research because they present ideas and information developed by scholars and specialists—and reviewed by scholars—for an audience of scholars. Magazines, in contrast, are commercial publications that present ideas and information for general readers who are nonspecialists; they provide nontechnical discussions and general reactions to issues. Newspapers, published daily or weekly, provide nearly instantaneous reactions to issues in primary stories and more reflective discussions in editorials and feature articles. These periodicals provide reports on research and discussions of contemporary ideas and issues of importance to writers of researched papers.

To cite periodicals in a reference list, follow the guidelines given in this chapter.

5a   An Article in a Journal With Continuous Paging

A journal with continuous paging numbers the pages of a volume consecutively, even though each issue of the journal has a separate number. For example, *Educational Psychologist*'s volume 44 (representing 2009) has numbered issues that are continuously paginated: issue number 1 (January) includes pages 1–71, number 2 (April) spans pages 73–157, number 3 (July) continues with pages 159–214, and so on.

When an article comes from a journal with continuous paging, list its author first, followed by the year of publication and the title of the article with sentence-style capitalization (without quotation marks). Next, include the title of the journal (with headline-style capitalization), a comma, the volume number, and another comma (all italicized). Finish the entry by listing the inclusive page numbers, without a page abbreviation.

Harrison, R. L., & Westwood, M. J. (2009). Preventing vicarious traumatization of mental health therapists: Identifying protective practices. *Psychotherapy: Theory, Research, Practice, Training, 46,* 203–219.

> ***In-text citation***   (Harrison & Westwood, 2009)

Nuttman-Shwartz, O. (2007). Is there life without work? *The International Journal of Aging and Human Development, 64,* 129–147.

> ***In-text citation***   (Nuttman-Shwartz, 2007)

5b   An Article in a Journal With Separate Paging

Although few current journals page their issues separately, some older journals may follow this pattern. A journal with separate paging begins each numbered issue with page 1, even though a group of issues is assigned a single volume number. For example, until recently, *Women and Health* numbered issues separately: Volume 44 (representing 2006–2007) began each issue on a new page: issue number 1 (2006) included pages 1–136, issue number 2 (2007) spanned pages 1–134, issue number 3 (2007) covered pages 1–122, and so on.

When a journal has separate paging for each issue, follow the volume number with the issue number, in parentheses; no space separates the volume from the issue, and the issue number and its parentheses are not italicized. All other information in the entry is the same as that of an entry for a journal with continuous paging.

Hughes, J. C., Brestan, E. V., Christens, B. D., Klinger, L. J., &
   Valle, L. A. (2004). Problem-solving interactions between
   mothers and children. *Child and Family Behavior
   Therapy, 26*(1), 1–16.

> ***First in-text citation***   (Hughes, Brestan, Christens,
> Klinger, & Valle, 2004)

> ***Subsequent citations***   (Hughes et al., 2004)

McDonald, T. P., Poertner, J., & Jennings, M. A. (2007). Permanency
   for children in foster care: A competing risks analysis. *The
   Journal of Social Science Research, 33*(4), 45–56.

> ***First in-text citation***   (McDonald, Poertner, &
> Jennings, 2007)

> ***Subsequent citations***   (McDonald et al., 2007)

5c   An Abstract

Although writers most often refer to entire articles, in very special circumstances (for example, when an abstract's summary
of key principles is succinct or quotable), you may want to cite
only the abstract. In those rare instances, first prepare a full
citation of the article; however, insert the word *Abstract,* not
italicized, within brackets after the article's title. The period
that normally follows the title follows the closing bracket.

Aten, J. D., Mangis, M. W., & Campbell, C. (2010). Psychotherapy
   with rural religious fundamentalist clients [Abstract].
   Journal of Clinical Psychology, 66, 513–523.

> ***In-text citation***   (Aten, Mangis, & Campbell, 2010)

Daniels, J. A., Bradley, M. C., Cramer, D. P., Winkler, A. T.,
   Kinebrew, K., & Crockett, D. (2007). The successful
   resolution of armed hostage/barricade events in schools:
   A qualitative analysis [Abstract]. *Psychology and the
   Schools, 44,* 601–613.

> ***In-text citation***   (Daniels et al., 2007)

5d   An Article in a Monthly Magazine

An article from a monthly magazine is listed by author. The
date is given by year and month, separated by a comma, in
parentheses. The article title appears next with sentence-style

capitalization. The title of the magazine, with headline-style capitalization, is followed by a comma, the volume number, and the issue number (if there is one). The entry ends with inclusive page numbers listed without page abbreviations. Note that only the year is included in the in-text citation, not the year and month.

Martinez-Conde, S., & Macknik, S. L. (2007, August). Windows on the mind. *Scientific American, 297*(2), 56–63.

> **In-text citation**   (Martinez-Conde & Macknik, 2007)

McGowen, K. (2009, July/August). Out of the past. *Discover, 30*(6), 30–37.

> **In-text citation**   (McGowen, 2009)

5e   An Article in a Weekly Magazine

The entry for a weekly magazine is identical to the entry for a monthly magazine except that the date of publication (along with the year and month) is included in parentheses. In the corresponding in-text citation, however, only the year is required.

Begley, S. (2010, February 8). The depressing news about antidepressants. *Newsweek, 155*(6), 34–41.

> **In-text citation**   (Begley, 2010)

Sacks, O. (2007, September 24). The abyss: Music and memory. *The New Yorker, 83*(28), 100–112.

> **In-text citation**   (Sacks, 2007)

5f   An Article in a Newspaper

An entry for a newspaper article resembles that for a magazine, except that section numbers or letters are included, and paging is indicated with a page abbreviation (*p.* or *pp.*, not italicized).

When sections are indicated by letters, they are presented along with the page numbers, without intervening punctuation or space. However, when newspaper sections are numbered, a colon separates the section from the page number.

Pogrebin, R. (2010, April 22). A mother's loss, a daughter's story. *The New York Times,* pp. E1, E9.

> **In-text citation**   (Pogrebin, 2010)

Notice that this article appears on nonconsecutive pages.

Rodriguez, A. (2007, September 16). When health care does more harm than good. *The Chicago Tribune*, p. 1:18.

> ***In-text citation***   (Rodriguez, 2007)

5g   An Article in a Newsletter

The entry for an article in a newsletter follows the pattern for a magazine: It includes the author, date, title of selection, title of newsletter, volume number, issue number, and inclusive pages (without page abbreviations). If a newsletter appears seasonally, include such identifying information along with the year (2008, spring).

Allen, R. (2007, April). Making science matter: Fresh approaches to teaching diverse students. *Education Update, 49*(4), 1, 6–8.

> ***In-text citation***   (Allen, 2007)

When pages are not sequential, list them all, separated by commas.

Golston, S. (2009, October). A failure of civil discourse. *The Social Studies Professional* (213), 3.

> ***In-text citation***   (Golston, 2009)

This newsletter is identified by volume number only.

5h   An Editorial

The entry for an editorial—an opinion-based essay— resembles that for a magazine or newspaper article, with one exception: The word *Editorial* (not italicized) is placed within brackets immediately after the title of the essay, if there is one. The period that normally follows the title follows the closing bracket.

Foner, E. (2010, April 5). Twisting history in Texas [Editorial]. *The Nation, 290*(13), 4–6.

> ***In-text citation***   (Foner, 2010)

Herbert, B. (2007, September 15). The nightmare is here [Editorial]. *The New York Times*, p. A29.

> ***In-text citation***   (Herbert, 2007)

5i   A Letter to the Editor

Following the author's name and the publication date, include the phrase *Letter to the editor* (not italicized) in brackets, followed by a period. The rest of the entry follows the pattern appropriate for the periodical.

Birch, M. A. (2007, September 3). [Letter to the editor]. *Fortune, 156,* 13.

> ***In-text citation***   (Birch, 2007)

Zietlow, Z. (2010, March). [Letter to the editor]. *Smithsonian, 40*(3), 5.

> ***In-text citation***   (Zietlow, 2010)

5j   A Review

After the author, date, and review title (if there is one), include a descriptive phrase that begins "Review of the book (motion picture, music recording, car, computer game)" and ends with the specific product name; enclose this information in brackets, followed by a period. Then continue the entry as is appropriate for the source.

Fox, B. (2006). [Review of the book *Ghosts of slavery: A literary archeology of black women's lives,* by J. Sharpe]. *African American Review, 40,* 838–839.

> ***In-text citation***   (Fox, 2006)

Schwarz, C. (2010, April). Quiet desperation. [Review of the book *Mrs. Bridge,* by E. S. Connell]. *The Atlantic, 300*(4), 87.

> ***In-text citation***   (Schwarz, 2010)

5k   An Abstract From *Dissertation Abstracts International*

This specialized entry requires the author's name, the year in parentheses, and the title of the dissertation (without quotation marks or italics). If you obtained the abstract from UMI (formerly University Microfilms), follow the title with *Dissertation Abstracts International* (italicized), the volume number, the issue number, and the page number.

If you obtained the dissertation from a university, place this information in parentheses: the phrase *Doctoral dissertation* (not italicized), the degree-granting university, and the year of completion—all separated with commas. Follow the closing parenthesis with a period. Complete the entry by identifying *Dissertation Abstracts International* (italicized), followed by the volume, issue, and the page number.

Markarian, G. (2005). Analyst forecasts, earnings management, and insider trading. *Dissertation Abstracts International, 66*(1), 237.

    In-text citation   (Markarian, 2005)

Vinski, E. J. (2007). Academic dishonesty and cognitive dissonance (Doctoral dissertation, City University of New York, 2007). *Dissertation Abstracts International, 67*(3), 117.

    In-text citation   (Vinski, 2007)

51 A Secondary Source

The authors of primary sources report their own research and ideas; the authors of secondary sources report the research and ideas of others. For example, an article by Lock, Couturier, Bryson, and Agras (2006) reported a multidimensional study that identified three major predictors of eating disorders; it is a primary source. Thompson-Brenner, Boisseau, and Satir (2010) incorporated material from Lock, Couturier, Bryson, and Agras in their article for *Journal of Clinical Psychology;* it is a secondary source. Although it is best to use the original or primary source (Lock, Couturier, Bryson, and Agras), at times you must use the secondary source (Thompson-Brenner, Boisseau, and Satir).

When you cite material that appears in a secondary source, the reference-list entry must be for *the source you used,* not the original (even though you might be able to secure full documentation from the secondary source's reference list). Refer to the original source in the text of the paper; however, in the in-text citation, clarify that you used the secondary source by including the phrase *as cited in* (not italicized). In the reference list, provide an entry for the secondary source.

Thompson-Brenner, H., Boisseau, C. L., & Satir, D. A. (2010).
Adolescent eating disorders: Treatment and response in a
naturalistic study. *Journal of Clinical Psychology, 66,*
277–301.

In-text discussion with citation　　Lock, Couturier, Bryson,
and Agras (2006) found that expected variables—like the
age of the client and the length of the treatment—did not
predict positive outcomes (as cited in Thompson-
Brenner, Boisseau, & Satir, 2010).

Citing Books and Other Separately Published Materials

Books provide comprehensive, extended discussions of topics. Those published by scholarly or university presses are often targeted to specialists in particular fields and provide a broad range of technical information and complex analyses.

Those published by trade (commercial) publishers are often directed to nonspecialists.

Because books take several years to produce, they frequently provide reflective interpretations that have the benefit of critical distance. Consequently, they provide balance in research.

To cite books in a reference list, follow the guidelines in this chapter.

6a   A Book by One Author

The entry for a book by a single author begins with his or her name, followed by the year in parentheses, the title, the city and state (or country), and the publisher. A book title is presented in italics, with sentence-style capitalization.

Chessick, R. D. (2007). *The future of psychoanalysis*. New York, NY: State University of New York Press.

> ***In-text citation***   (Chessick, 2007)

Weiner, M. F. (2010). *Power, protest, and the public school: Jewish and African American struggles in New York City*. New Brunswick, NJ: Rutgers University Press.

> ***In-text citation***   (Weiner, 2010)

6b   A Book by Two or More Authors

When a book has multiple authors, their names appear in the order presented on the title page, not alphabetical order. The names of two to seven authors are listed, with all of their names inverted. An ampersand (&) joins the last two names. If a book has eight or more authors, the first six are listed, followed by ellipsis points (three spaced periods) and the name of the last author.

Lazarus, R. S., & Lazarus, B. N. (2006). *Coping with aging*. New York, NY: Oxford University Press.

> ***In-text citation***   (Lazarus & Lazarus, 2006)

Wright, J. P., Tibbetts, S. G., & Daigle, L. E. (2008). *Criminals in the making: Criminality across the life course*. Thousand Oaks, CA: Sage.

> ***In-text citation***   (Wright, Tibbetts, & Daigle, 2008)

6c A Book With No Author Named

When no author or editor is named, list the book by title. When an editor is listed, begin with the editor's name. The following source is listed by title.

United Press International stylebook and guide to newswriting (4th ed.). (2004). Herndon, VA: Capital Books.

> **In-text citation** (*United Press International*, 2004)

The edition number follows the title, in parentheses; notice that the edition number is not italicized and that the period follows the closing parenthesis. With an authorless book, the year follows the title or edition number. (See 6e for the common pattern of presenting editions.)

The following source is listed by editor.

VandenBos, G. R. (Ed.). (2007). *APA dictionary of psychology.* Washington, DC: American Psychological Association.

> **In-text citation** (VandenBos, 2007)

6d A Book With an Organization as Author

When an organization is listed as the author, spell out the name completely in the author position. When the organization is also the publisher, use the word *Author,* not italicized, in the publisher position.

American Psychological Association. (2009). *Publication manual of the American Psychological Association* (6th ed.). Washington, DC: Author.

> **First in-text citation** (American Psychological Association [APA], 2009)

> **Subsequent citations** (APA, 2009)

The first in-text citation with an organization as an author includes the full name, followed by the abbreviated name within brackets; additional references include only the abbreviated name.

American Medical Association. (2007). *American Medical Association manual of style: A guide to authors and editors* (10th ed.). New York, NY: Oxford University Press.

> **First in-text citation** (American Medical Association [AMA], 2007)

> **Subsequent citations** (AMA, 2007)

6e   An Edition Other Than the First

The edition number, which appears on the title page, follows the title of the book, in parentheses. Note that it is not italicized and that the period that normally follows the title follows the closing parenthesis instead.

Moritsugu, J., Wong, F. Y., & Duffy, K. G. (2010). *Community psychology* (4th ed.). Boston, MA: Allyn.

> **In-text citation**   (Moritsugu, Wong, & Duffy, 2010)

Young, M. E., & Long, L. L. (2007). *Counseling and therapy for couples* (2nd ed.). Belmont, CA: Brooks–Cole.

> **In-text citation**   (Young & Long, 2007)

Note that dual publishers are both listed, separated by an en dash or a hyphen.

6f   An Edited Collection

Present an entire edited collection like a traditional book, with the editor's name in the author position.

Foreman, M. D., Milisen, K., & Fulner, T. T. (Eds.). (2010). *Critical care nursing of older adults: Best practices.* New York, NY: Springer.

> **In-text citation**   (Foreman, Milisen, & Fulner, 2010)

Gilde, C. (Ed.). (2007). *Higher education: Open for business.* Lanham, MD: Lexington Books.

> **In-text citation**   (Gilde, 2007)

6g   An Original Selection in an Edited Collection

To cite an original selection in an edited collection, begin with the name of the author of the selection, followed by the date in parentheses and the selection's title (with sentence-style capitalization and no quotation marks). Introduced by the word *In* (not italicized), the collection editor is listed next (his or her name is in normal order, followed by the abbreviation *Ed.* in parentheses, not italicized), followed by a comma. The title of the collection, italicized, is followed by the inclusive page numbers for the selection, with the abbreviation for pages, listed in parentheses. The entry ends with the facts of publication.

Estrin, M., & Malm, C. (2010). State weakness and infectious diseases. In S. E. Rice, C. Graff, & C. Pascul (Eds.), *Confronting poverty: Weak states and U.S. national security* (pp. 167–201). Washington, DC: Brookings Institution Press.

> ***In-text citation***   (Estrin & Malm, 2010)

Royzman, E. B., McCauley, C., & Rozin, P. (2005). From Plato to Putnam: Four ways to think about hate. In R. J. Sternberg (Ed.), *The psychology of hate* (pp. 3–35). Washington, DC: American Psychological Association.

> ***In-text citation***   (Royzman, McCauley, & Rozin, 2005)

6h   A Previously Published Selection in an Edited Collection

When a selection has been reprinted from a work published earlier, provide identifying information in parentheses at the end of the entry. Include the information for the original source, but notice that page numbers appear with the abbreviation for pages (even when the original source is a periodical), and the year follows the page numbers. Also note that the closing parenthesis is not followed by a period.

Bazemore, G., & Day, S. E. (2005). Restoring the balance: Juvenile and community justice. In D. L. Parry (Ed.), *Essential readings in juvenile justice* (pp. 405–414). Upper Saddle River, NJ: Pearson. (Reprinted from *Juvenile Justice, 3*(1), pp. 3–14, 1996)

> ***In-text citation***   (Bazemore & Day, 2005)

Soames, S. (2009). The necessary argument. In *Philosophical essays: Vol. 1. Natural language: What it means and how we use it* (pp. 202–207). Princeton, NJ: Princeton University Press. (Reprinted from *Linguistics and Philosophy 14*, pp. 575–580, 1991)

> ***In-text citation***   (Soames, 2009)

This reprinted essay appears in the first volume of a multivolume work (see 6k).

6i   A Revised or Enlarged Edition

Enclose the description of a revised or enlarged edition in parentheses following the title. As with other editions, the parenthetical information precedes the period that follows the title. This information is not italicized.

Benardot, D. (2006). *Advanced sports nutrition* (Rev. ed.). Champaign, IL: Human Kinetics.

    In-text citation   (Benardot, 2006)

Street, N. L., & Matelski, M. J. (2008). *American businesses in China: Balancing culture and communication* (Rev. ed.). Jefferson, NC: McFarland.

    In-text citation   (Street & Matelski, 2008)

6j   A Reprinted Book

The entry for a reprinted book begins with the full entry of the version you have used; the entry ends with a parenthetical description of the original publication date, with no period after the closing parenthesis. Note that the in-text citation includes both dates, presented in chronological order, separated by a slash.

Kimmel, A. J. (2007). *Ethical issues in behavioral research: Basic and applied perspectives*. Malden, MA: Blackwell. (Original work published 1966)

    In-text citation   (Kimmel, 1966/2007)

Momaday, N. S. (2009). *In the presence of the sun: Stories and poems, 1961–1991*. Albuquerque, NM: University of New Mexico. (Original work published 1992)

    In-text citation   (Momaday, 1992/2009)

6k   A Multivolume Work

When citing a complete multivolume work, the number of volumes appears in parentheses following the title but before the period; if an edition number is required, it precedes the volume number.

Fisher, B. S., & Lab, S. P. (Eds.). (2010). *Encyclopedia of victimology and crime prevention* (Vols. 1–2). Thousand Oaks, CA: Sage.

> ***In-text citation***   (Fisher & Lab, 2010)

When citing a separately titled volume of a multivolume work, list the multivolume title first, followed by a colon and one space. Then list the separate volume number, followed by a period, and the single volume title. The multivolume title, volume information, and specific title are all italicized. Note that the names of series editors precede those of volume editors; the order of presentation, then, corresponds to the order of the titles.

Osherson, D. N. (Series Ed.), Scarborough, D., & Sternberg, S. (Vol. Eds.). (1998). *An invitation to cognitive science: Vol. 4. Methods, models, and conceptual issues* (2nd ed.). Cambridge, MA: MIT Press.

> ***In-text citation***   (Osherson, Scarborough, & Sternberg, 1999)

---

61   An Article in an Encyclopedia or Other Reference Work

To cite an article in an encyclopedia or other reference work, begin with the author's name, when it is available, followed by the date in parentheses. Next list the subject heading under which the material appears (exactly as it appears in the source), without special punctuation. Follow it with the title of the reference work. In parentheses, but before the period that follows the title, include the volume number, if applicable, and the inclusive pages. End the entry with the city and state (or country) and the publisher.

   When a reference work has a large editorial board, include the first editor's name and *et al.* (not italicized) to substitute for the other editors' names.

Barber, C. (2009). Gender identity. In E. M. Anderman & L. H. Anderman (Eds.), *Psychology of classroom learning: An encyclopedia* (Vols. 1–2, pp. 428–430). Detroit, MI: Gale–Cengage.

> ***In-text citation***   (Barber, 2009)

Sulloway, F. J. (2007). Birth order and sibling competition.
In R. I. M. Dunbar & L. Barrett (Eds.), *Oxford handbook
of evolutionary psychology* (pp. 297–311). New York, NY:
Oxford University Press.

> ***In-text citation***   (Sullaway, 2007)

6m   A Work in a Series

If a book is part of a series, that fact is stated on the title page
or the facing page. The entry follows the pattern for a similar
book, except that the series title (italicized, with headline-
style capitalization) appears in a phrase preceding the city
and publisher.

Friedman, D. (2010). *Historical building construction: Design,
materials, and technology* (2nd ed.). In *Building History
Series*. New York, NY: Norton.

> ***In-text citation***   (Friedman, 2010)

Nelson, S. J. (2007). *Leaders in the labyrinth: College presidents
and the battleground of creeds and convictions*. In *Praeger
Series on Higher Education*. Westport, CT:
Praeger–Greenwood.

> ***In-text citation***   (Nelson, 2007)

6n   A Translation

Under most circumstances, the translator of a text is cited
in parentheses immediately after the title of the selection
(whether it is an essay, chapter, or complete text) but before
the closing period for that element.

de Beauvoir, S. (2003). The married woman (H. M. Parshly,
Trans.). In S. Hirschberg & T. Hirschberg (Eds.), *Past to
present: Ideas that changed our world* (pp. 188–194).
Upper Saddle River, NJ: Prentice Hall.

> ***In-text citation***   (de Beauvoir, 2003)

The previous example indicates that Parshly translated only
the selection presented in this entry. Had he translated the
entire collection, his name would have appeared after the
anthology's title.

Tram, D. T. (2007). *Last night I dreamed of peace: The diary of Dang Thuy Tram* (A. X. Pham, Trans.). New York, NY: Harmony Books.

> **In-text citation**   (Pham, 2007)

This entry indicates that Pham translated the entire book.

6o A Government Document—Committee, Commission, Department

An entry for a government document follows the pattern used for another similar source. Because many government documents are book-length, that pattern most often applies. Note, however, that APA style requires a publication number for a government document, if available (usually found on the title page or back cover), presented in parentheses after the title; the document number is not italicized. When serving as publisher, the *U.S. Government Printing Office* is spelled out, not abbreviated, and not italicized.

Greenberg, E., Dunleavy, E., & Kutner, M. (2007). *Literacy behind bars: Results from the 2003 national assessment of adult literacy prison survey* (NCES 2007–473). Washington, DC: National Center for Educational Statistics.

> **In-text citation**   (Greenberg, Dunleavy, & Kutner, 2007)

National Archives and Records Administration. (2004). *Federal records pertaining to Brown v. Board of Education of Topeka, Kansas (1954)* (Reference Information Paper 112). Washington, DC: Author.

> **First in-text citation**   (National Archives and Records Administration [NARA], 2004)

> **Subsequent citations**   (NARA, 2004)

6p A Preface, Introduction, Foreword, Epilogue, or Afterword

When introductory or closing material is titled, it is presented like a selection in a collection; however, a descriptive word (*Preface, Epilogue,* and so on, not italicized) is enclosed within brackets before the period. Cite pages as they appear in the source, using either lower-case Roman or Arabic numerals.

Untitled material is cited separately by providing a descriptive title (within brackets), followed by complete entry information.

Kassel, J. D., & Veilleux, J. C. (2010). The complex interplay between substance abuse and emotion [Introduction]. In J. D. Kassel (Ed.), Substance abuse and emotion (pp. 3–12). Washington, DC: American Psychological Association.

In-text citation (Kassel & Veilleux, 2010)

Nieto, S. (2007). The national mythology and urban teaching [Introduction]. In G. Campano, *Immigrant students and literacy: Reading, writing, and remembering* (pp. 1–6). New York, NY: Teachers College Press.

In-text citation (Nieto, 2007)

6q A Monograph

To create an entry for a monograph (a separately published, essay-length selection that is sometimes a reprint of a journal article and sometimes an independently prepared selection that is part of a series), include traditional publishing information. However, after the title and in parentheses, include the monograph series title and monograph number, if available; the monograph number is introduced by *No.,* the abbreviation for *number.*

Brown, R., & Stobart, K. (2008). *Understanding boundaries and containment in clinical practice* (Society of Analytical Psychology Monograph). London, England: Karnac.

In-text citation (Brown & Stobart, 2008)

Checkoway, H., Pearce, N., & Kriebel, D. (Eds.). (2004). *Research methods in occupational epidemiology* (2nd ed., Monographs in Epidemiology and Biostatistics No. 34). New York, NY: Oxford University Press.

In-text citation (Checkoway, Pearce, & Kriebel, 2004)

6r A Pamphlet or Brochure

When a pamphlet or brochure contains clearly presented information, it is cited like a book, with a descriptive title enclosed in brackets. When information is missing, use these abbreviations: *N.p.* for "No place of publication," *n.p.* for "no publisher," and *n.d.* for "no date." None of these abbreviations is italicized in an entry.

Gable, S. (2008). *Nurturing children's talents* [Pamphlet].
   Columbia, MO: University of Missouri. (Original work
   published 1999)

   In-text citation   (Gable, 1999/2008)

This reprinted pamphlet requires information about the original publication (see 6j).

*Loving your family, feeding their future: Nutrition education
   through the food stamp program* [Pamphlet]. (2007).
   Washington, DC: Food and Nutrition Service, U.S.
   Department of Agriculture.

   In-text citation   (*Loving Your Family*, 2007)

This authorless work uses a shortened version of the title in the in-text citation.

6s   A Dissertation

A published dissertation is a book and should be cited accordingly (see 6a). The entry for an unpublished dissertation begins with the author's name, the date, and the title, presented in the pattern used for a book. In parentheses, include the phrase *Unpublished doctoral dissertation* (not italicized), followed by a period. Then provide the name of the degree-granting university, followed by a comma and the city and state (or country).

Hall, E. M. (2007). *Posttraumatic stress symptoms in parents
   of children with injuries.* (Unpublished doctoral
   dissertation). Boston University, Boston, MA.

   In-text citation   (Hall, 2007)

Smertek, K. (2009). *Art, commerce, and scholarship in the Age of
   Enlightenment: Pierre-Jean Mariette and the making of art
   history.* (Unpublished doctoral dissertation). University of
   Delaware, Newark, DE.

   In-text citation   (Smertek, 2009)

6t Published Proceedings From a Conference

The published proceedings from a conference present revised, printed versions of papers that were delivered at the meeting. If the proceedings are published individually, cite them as books. If they are published regularly, present them as periodicals.

Capitalize the name of the meeting or conference. If the title includes the state, province, or country, do not repeat it in the publishing information.

Bahl-Nielsen, B. (2006). Mirrors, body image, and self. In E. Zacharacoponlou (Ed.), *Beyond the mind–body dualism: Psychoanalysis and the human body: Proceedings of the 6th Delphi International Symposium* (pp. 87–94). San Diego, CA: Elsevier.

In-text citation (Bahl-Nielsen, 2006)

Knepshield, L. J. (2009). Encouraged to apply: Diversity and the scholarship process. In S. McCray (Ed.), *Leading the way: Student engagement and nationally competitive awards* (pp. 67–74). Fayetteville, AK: University of Arkansas Press.

In-text citation (Knepshield, 2009)

The Fourth National Conference for the National Association of Fellowship Advisors was held in 2007; the printed version of the proceedings appeared in 2009.

6u Multiple Works by the Same Author

When citing several sources by the same author, repeat the name completely each time. Alphabetical order takes precedence, with single authors listed before multiple authors. List works by single authors or by the same multiple authors chronologically. If works are published in the same year, arrange them alphabetically by title.

Sternberg, R. J. (1990). *Metaphors of the mind: Conceptions of the nature of intelligence.* New York, NY: Cambridge University Press.

Sternberg, R. J. (Ed.). (2003). *Psychologists defying the crowd: Stories of those who battled the establishment and won.* Washington, DC: American Psychological Association.

Sternberg, R. J. (2003). *Why smart people can be so stupid.* New Haven, CT: Yale University Press.

Sternberg, R. J. (2007). *Wisdom, intelligence, and creativity synthesized.* New York, NY: Cambridge University Press.

Sternberg, R. J., & Grigorenko, E. L. (2000). *Teaching for successful intelligence: To increase student learning and achievement* (2nd ed.). Arlington Heights, IL: Skylight.

Sternberg, R. J, & Grigorenko, E. L. (2003). *The psychology of abilities, competencies, and expertise.* New York, NY: Cambridge University Press.

Alternative in-text citations

- The 1990 book: (Sternberg, 1990)
- The first 2003 book: (Sternberg, 2003a)
- The second 2003 book: (Sternberg, 2003b)
- All four single-author works in the same citation: (Sternberg, 1990, 2003a, 2003b, 2007)
- The first multiple-author book: (Sternberg & Grigorenko, 2000)
- The second multiple-author book: (Sternberg & Grigorenko, 2007)
- A combination of sources in the same citation: (Sternberg, 1990, 2007; Sternberg & Grigorenko, 2003)

Sternberg's four separately written works appear first, arranged in chronological order and then alphabetically by title. The Sternberg and Grigorenko books follow, again in chronological order.

6v A Secondary Source

The authors of primary sources report their own research and ideas; the authors of secondary sources report the research and ideas of others. For example, Tomasello (1992) conducted a study of young children's language acquisition and reported it in a journal article; it is a primary source. Nelson (2007) incorporated material from the original article in her book *Young Minds in Social Worlds: Experience, Meaning, and Memory;* it is a secondary source. Although it is best to use the original or primary source (Tomasello), sometimes you must use the secondary source (Nelson).

When you cite material that appears in a secondary source, the reference-list entry must be for *the source you used,* not the original (even though you might be able to secure full documentation from the secondary source's reference list).

Refer to the original source in the text of the paper; however, in the in-text citation, clarify that you used the secondary source by including the phrase *as cited in* (not italicized). In the reference list, provide an entry for the secondary source.

Nelson, K. (2007). *Young minds in social worlds: Experience, meaning, and memory*. Cambridge, MA: Harvard University Press.

> ***In-text reference and citation***   Tomasello (1992) asserted that children learn words within usage-based, grammatical contexts (as cited in Nelson, 2007).

Audiovisual sources—motion pictures, recordings, speeches, works of art, and other visual images—are used infrequently in APA papers. Nevertheless, they can provide interesting support for discussions and create variety within a paper.

To cite an audiovisual source in a reference list, follow the guidelines in this chapter.

7a A Motion Picture

An entry for a motion picture begins with the producer's or director's name (with the word *Producer* or *Director* in parentheses but not italicized), followed by the year of the motion picture's release, its title (italicized, with sentence-style capitalization), and a descriptive title (in brackets). The entry ends with the country of origin and the company.

Include other people's contributions after the motion picture title (in brackets), using brief phrases (*Narr. by, With, Written by*—not italicized) to clarify their roles.

Kenner, R., & Pearlstein, E. (Producers). (2009). *Food, inc.*
[Motion picture]. [With G. Hirschberg, M. Pollan, J. Salatin, & E. Schlosser]. United States: Magnolia Pictures.

In-text citation   (Kenner & Pearlstein, 2009)

Pakula, A. J., Barish, K., Gerrity, W. C., & Starger, M. (Producers), & Pakula, A. J. (Director). (1982). *Sophie's choice* [Motion picture]. [With M. Streep, K. Kline, & P. MacNichol]. United States: Universal.

> ***In-text citation***   (Pakula, Barish, Gerrity, & Starger, 1982)

7b   A Slide Set or Filmstrip

A slide set (either photographic slides or those prepared in PowerPoint or other digital formats) or a filmstrip is cited just as a motion picture is, with one exception: Include a descriptive title, such as *Slide set,* in brackets (but not italicized) after the title.

Determined accord: Pandemic preparedness workshop for community managers [Slide set]. (2009). Washington, DC: U.S. Department of Homeland Security–Federal Emergency Management Agency.

> ***In-text citation***   (*Determined Accord,* 2009)

Because the source had no producer or director, the citation begins with the title. The in-text citation uses a shortened version of the title.

Technical Working Group for Eyewitness Evidence. (2003). *Eyewitness evidence: A trainer's manual for law enforcement* (NCJ 188678) [Slides]. United States: U.S. Department of Justice.

> ***First in-text citation***   (Technical Working Group for Eyewitness Evidence [TWGEE], 2003)

> ***Subsequent citations***   (TWGEE, 2003)

As a government document, this entry incorporates a publication number after the title of the slide series.

7c   A Television Broadcast

A regular television program is listed by producer or director, broadcast date (which may be either a year or a specific broadcast date), program title (italicized, with sentence-style capitalization), a descriptive phrase (in brackets), the city and state (or country), and the network (spelled out completely). Include other people's contributions after the program title (in brackets), using brief phrases (*Narr. by, With, Written by*— not italicized) to clarify their roles.

Newman, L. (Producer). (2010). *Scrubs* [Television series].
[With Z. Braff, D. Faison, M. Mosley, K. Bishe, J. C.
McGinley, E. Coupe, & D. Franco]. New York, NY:
National Broadcasting Company.

> ***In-text citation***   (Newman, 2010)

To refer to an individual episode, cite the writer and director,
the specific broadcast date, the episode title without special
punctuation, and a descriptive phrase in brackets. Then, use
the word *In* (not italicized) to introduce the program title. The
rest of the entry follows normal patterns.

Moran, T. L. (Writer), & Yaiyanes, G. (Director). (2009, October
12). Instant karma [Television series episode]. [With H.
Laurie, R. S. Leonard, & L. Edelstein]. In *House*. Los
Angeles, CA: Fox Broadcasting Company.

> ***In-text citation***   (Moran & Yaiyanes, 2009)

Note that only the year appears in the in-text citation.

7d   A Radio Broadcast

An entry for a radio broadcast follows the guidelines for a
television broadcast; however, note that a radio station's
call numbers are listed. When a broadcast does not have an
assigned title, add a descriptive phrase in brackets.

Murrow, E. R. (1940, September 13). [Radio broadcast]. New
York, NY: WCBS.

> ***In-text citation***   (Murrow, 1940)

7e   A Recording

An entry for an entire recording begins with the writer–
composer's name, the date of the recording, and the album
title (in italics, with sentence-style capitalization), with the
recording format in brackets. The entry ends with the city and
state (or country), and distribution company.

The Beatles. (2009). *Abbey Road* (Remastered) [CD]. Hollywood,
CA–London, England: Capital–EMI. (Original work
released 1969)

> ***In-text citation***   (The Beatles, 1969/2009)

A remastered recording, like a revised or reprinted book, requires a clarification in parentheses, as well as a parenthetical statement about the original release. Both release dates are included in the in-text citation.

To emphasize a single selection on a recording, begin with the writer–composer and the date, followed by the title of the brief work (with sentence-style capitalization but without special punctuation). Using the word *On* (not italicized), include the title of the complete recording and other production information. Include the track number in the in-text citation.

Winehouse, A. (2006). Rehab. On *Back to black* [CD]. New York, NY: Universal Records.

> ***In-text citation***   (Winehouse, 2006, track 1)

7f   An Interview

An interview is a personal communication. As such, it is not included in a reference list. However, it is cited in the text of the paper by enclosing the phrase *personal communication* (not italicized) and the date in parentheses. Notice that initials are required with the name.

> Double-blind studies are necessary to ensure the validity of research (K. J. Kalb, personal communication, March 4, 2010).

7g   A Transcript

A transcript entry describes the source of an original broadcast, with clarifying information in brackets, and information about availability.

Gupta, S. (2010, April 18). Addiction: Life on the edge. In *CNN Presents* [Television series episode]. [Transcript]. Atlanta, GA: Cable News Network. Available: CNN Transcripts.

> ***In-text citation***   (Gupta, 2010)

Simon, S. (Host). (2010, April 10). What your voice tells people about you [Radio broadcast]. [With D. Hicks]. [Transcript]. Washington, DC: National Public Radio. Available: NPR Transcripts.

> ***In-text citation***   (Simon, 2010)

7h A Lecture or Speech

An entry for a lecture or speech includes the speaker's name, the date of the speech, the title of the speech (italicized) or a descriptive title (in brackets), a series title or a description of the speech-making context, and the location (most often, the city and state or country).

Nixon, R. (1974, August 8). [Resignation speech]. Speech presented at the White House, Washington, DC.

> **In-text citation**   (Nixon, 1974)

Robinson, M. (2009, April 12). *Human rights strategies in the 21st century.* Lecture presented for the Stanford Presidential Lectures in Humanities and Arts, Stanford University, Stanford, CA.

> **In-text citation**   (Robinson, 2009)

7i A Work of Art

An entry for a work of art includes the artist's name, the completion date, the title (either assigned by the artist or attributed), a description of the medium (enclosed in brackets), the museum or collection name, and the city (and state or country, if necessary). When artists assign titles, they are italicized; do not italicize titles that other people have assigned to the work.

Hopper, E. (1930). *Early Sunday morning* [Oil on canvas]. Whitney Museum of American Art, New York, NY.

> **In-text citation**   (Hopper, 1930)

Healy, G. P. A. (1887). Abraham Lincoln [Oil on canvas]. National Portrait Gallery, Washington, DC.

> **In-text citation**   (Healy, 1887)

Healy, the artist, did not formally title this painting. "Abraham Lincoln" is the attributed title and, therefore, is not italicized.

7j A Map, Graph, Table, or Chart

Often prepared as part of another source, a map, graph, table, or chart is most often treated like a selection in an edited collection (or a chapter in a book). If known, include the name of the author, artist, or designer responsible for the element, followed by the publication date, in parentheses. Include the title, with sentence-style capitalization but without special punctuation. Follow the title with a descriptive label in brackets, followed by a period. Then include entry information required for the source. When a map, graph, table, or chart is prepared independently, it is treated like a book.

Feistritzer, C. E., & Haar, C. K. (2008). Number of alternative routes to teacher certification in each state (2006) [Map]. In C. E. Feistritzer & C. K. Haar, *Alternative routes to teaching* (p. 4). Upper Saddle River, NJ: Pearson.

> ***In-text citation***　　(Feistritzer & Haar, 2008)

National Institutes of Health. (2007). Recent NIH budget appropriations [Chart]. In R. I. Field, *Health care regulation in America: Complexity, confrontation, and compromise* (p. 212). New York, NY: Oxford University Press.

> ***First in-text citation***　　(National Institutes of Health [NIH], 2007)

> ***Subsequent citations***　　(NIH, 2007)

Citing Electronic Sources

The Internet provides researchers with access to an amazing array of resources. Many periodicals are now available in electronic, as well as print, form. Books—out-of-print volumes, as well as recent publications—are accessible online. Documents, correspondence, photographs, films, recordings, and a host of other resource materials are available online in digitized form. Because these sources are available anywhere that a researcher can establish an Internet connection, research is no longer a local activity, restricted to the nearby library, lab, or collection. Instead, researchers can access a far broader range of materials than they once could.

Take advantage of the wealth of online material but be aware that citing these resources sometimes requires ingenuity because citation information can be difficult to locate.

To cite online sources in a reference list, follow the guidelines in this chapter.

Principles for Citing Electronic Sources

1. *Follow patterns for print sources when possible.* Use reference-list entries for similar print sources as your guide: Include as much of the information that is required for corresponding print versions as you can locate and present the information in the same order and format.

2. *Provide retrieval information.* After providing basic information about an online source—author, date, title, and so on—add sufficient retrieval information so that readers can locate your sources on the Internet. Use retrieval dates *only* when sources are likely to change (for example, wikis).

3. *Use a Digital Object Identifier (DOI) when available.* Current publications usually display the DOI—a fixed alphanumeric link to an online document—at the top of the first page. When it is available, use it to identify the source.

4. *Use a Uniform Resource Locator (URL) as an alternative.* When a DOI is not available, use the URL of the home page of the online source. A complete URL is necessary *only* when a source is difficult to locate within a website.

5. *Present a source's DOI or URL with care.* To ensure that you record a DOI or URL exactly, copy and paste it into your reference-list entry.

6. Divide the DOI or URL when necessary. To avoid large spaces in citations, divide DOIs or URLs *before* punctuation; however, retain *http://* as a unit.

7. *Present retrieval statements with care.* A retrieval statement ending with a DOI or a URL has no end punctuation, because a closing period might be misinterpreted as part of the identification number or electronic address.

Retrieval Statements

Kind of source	Pattern for retrieval statement
A source with a Digital Object Identifier (DOI)	doi:10.1022/0012-9142. 76.3.482
A source with a home page URL	Retrieved from http://www. childdevelopmentinfo.com
An abstract (A phrase ending in a database name is followed by a period; a phrase ending in a URL has no closing period.)	Abstract retrieved from Wiley Education database.
	Abstract retrieved from http://www.ncjrs.gov
A source from an organizational or professional website	Retrieved from the American Psychological Association website: http://www.apa.org/

As you gather information to cite electronic sources, your goal should be to provide the most complete set of information possible for each electronic source, following the guidelines in this chapter.

Specialized Online Sources

Online sources exist in many forms. Although they are all designed in approximately the same way—with a home page that directs users to subpages where information can be found—some specialized sites have distinct purposes and applications.

- *Professional websites.* Affiliated with professional organizations in virtually every discipline, these sites provide materials that support or enhance the work of the organization—research documents, online resources, web links, news items, press releases, and so on. Website titles typically include the organization's name, but if they do not, this information may be added for clarity.

(cont. on next page)

Specialized Online Sources

- *Information databases.*   Typically developed by information-technology firms or government agencies, these sites provide access to cataloged information that is accessed by using keyword search terms. Periodical databases like ProQuest, EBSCOhost, LexisNexis, JSTOR, and WorldCat make periodical articles available in a variety of formats (see 1d); other databases provide access to cataloged music, art, historical documents, and so on. When the database name is included in a URL, it does not have to be listed separately in a reference-list entry; however, when the URL includes only an acronym, it is often helpful to provide the name for additional clarity.

- *Scholarly projects.*   Often affiliated with universities, foundations, and government agencies, these sites are depositories of resources as varied as articles, books, digitized images of original documents, sound recordings, and film clips. Because their affiliations help establish their credibility, that information is sometimes included in reference-list entries.

8a   An Article in an Online Journal

To cite an article in an online journal, first provide the information that is required for the print version of the article (see 5a and 5b). Then close the entry with a retrieval statement. If the article has a DOI, use that number. If it does not, present a retrieval statement that is appropriate for the kind of online source (see page 107).

Orth, U., Trzesniewski, K. H., & Robbins, R. W. (2010). Self-esteem development from young adulthood to old age: A cohort-sequential longitudinal study. *Journal of Personality and Social Psychology, 98,* 645–658. doi: 10.1037/a0018769

> *In-text citation*   (Orth, Trzesniewski, & Robbins, 2010)

Renn, K. A. (2009). Education policy, politics, and mixed-heritage students in the United States. *Journal of Social Issues, 65,* 165–183. doi: 10.1111.1540-4560.2008.01593.x

> *In-text citation*   (Renn, 2009)

8b An Article in an Online Magazine

Articles in online magazines are presented in the same ways as those in online journals, except that dates may also include days and months (see 5d and 5e). Follow similar patterns to present reference-list entries.

Kluger, J. (2007, October 17). The power of birth order. *Time, 170*(18), 42–48. Retrieved from http://www.time.com

In-text citation (Kluger, 2007)

Miller, G. (2010, May). How our brains make memories. *Smithsonian.* Retrieved from http://www.smithsonianmag. com

No volume, issue, or page information is available for this source.

In-text citation (Miller, 2010)

8c An Article in an Online Newspaper

To cite an article in an online newspaper, first provide the information that is required for the print version of the article (see 5f) but exclude section designations and page numbers. Then present a retrieval statement that is appropriate for the kind of online source (see page 107).

Gettleman, J. (2007, December 27). UN says malnutrition in Darfur on the rise. *Boston Globe.* Retrieved from http://www.boston.com

In-text citation (Gettleman, 2007)

Glionna, J. M. (2010, May 1). Without words, speaking different languages. *Los Angeles Times.* Retrieved from http://www. latimes.com

In-text citation (Glionna, 2010)

8d An Article in an Online Newsletter

An entry for an online newsletter follows the same pattern as that for an online newspaper. However, because newsletter articles are sometimes difficult to locate, include the complete URL for your source.

Keith, D. (2007, October). Test your leadership skills: Do you
    have what it takes? *Team Strategies for Business Leaders*.
    Retrieved from http://www.mlevelsystems.com/
    October2007/Newsletter.pdf/

    In-text citation   (Keith, 2007)

Truog, R. D. (2009, fall). Brain death and the dead-donor rule:
    A critique and alternatives. *Newsletter on Philosophy and
    Medicine, 9*(1), 18–22. Retrieved from http://www.apaonline.
    org/documents/publications/vo9n1_Medicine.pdf

    In-text citation   (Truog, 2010)

8e An Online Book

To cite an online book, first prepare a standard entry (see 6a
to 6q); however, omit the city and publisher. Then provide the
retrieval statement.

Pierce, R. V. (1895). *The people's common sense medical advisor
    in plain English, or medicine simplified* (54th ed.).
    Retrieved from http://www.gutenberg.org/catalog

    In-text citation   (Pierce, 1895)

Prothrow-Stith, D., & Spivak, H. R. (2004). *Murder is no accident:
    Understanding and preventing youth violence in America*.
    Retrieved from http://www.questia.com

    In-text citation   (Prothrow-Stith & Spivak, 2004)

8f An Online Dissertation

To cite an online dissertation, include author, date, and title,
followed by the phrase *Doctoral dissertation* (not italicized)
in parentheses. Close the entry with a retrieval statement that
includes the name of the database and, if available, the accession or order number in parentheses.

AbuDagg, A. (2009). A multilevel analysis of organizational and
    market predictors of patient assessments of inpatient
    hospital care (Doctoral dissertation). Retrieved from
    Pennsylvania State University's electronic Theses and
    Dissertations Archive: http://etda.libraries.psu.edu

    In-text citation   (AbuDagg, 2009)

Aultman-Bettridge, T. (2007). A gender-specific analysis of community-based juvenile justice reform: The effectiveness of family therapy programs for delinquent girls (Doctoral dissertation). Retrieved from ProQuest Dissertations and Theses. (UMI No. AAT 3267887)

> *In-text citation*   (Aultman-Bettridge, 2007)

8g   An Online Abstract

To cite an abstract of an article in an online journal or an abstract from an online service, first provide the information that is required for the print version of an abstract (see 5c). Then provide a retrieval statement that is appropriate for your source; you may include an accession number in parentheses at the end of the entry.

Borius, M., Holzapfel, S., Tudiver, F., & Bader, E. (2007, December). Counseling and psychotherapy skills training for family physicians [Abstract]. *Families, Systems, and Health, 25*, 382–391. Retrieved from http://www.apa.org/psycharticles

> *In-text citation*   (Borius, Holzapfel, Tudiver, & Bader, 2007)
> *Subsequent citations*   (Borius et al., 2007)

Saxon, D., Ricketts, T., & Heywood, J. (2010). Who drops out? Do measures of risk to self and to others predict unplanned endings in primary care counseling [Abstract]? *Counseling and Psychotherapy Research, 10*(1), 13–21. Abstract retrieved from Informaworld.com

> *In-text citation*   (Saxon, Ricketts, & Heywood, 2010)

8h   An Article in an Online Encyclopedia or Other Reference Work

To cite an article from an online encyclopedia or reference work, first provide the information required for a print source (see 6l). Then include a retrieval statement.

Intelligence. (2010). In *Merriam–Webster's online dictionary*. Retrieved from http://www.merriam-webster.com/dictionary/

> *In-text citation*   ("Intelligence," 2010)

Sternberg, R. J. (2010). Intelligence, human. In
　　Encyclopaedia Britannica online. Retrieved from
　　http://search.eb.com

　In-text citation　(Sternberg, 2010)

8i　A Professional Website, Information Database, or Scholarly Project

If you refer to an entire professional website, information database, or scholarly project, you do not need to include an entry in your reference list. However, you must identify the title of the source clearly in the text of your paper (capitalized but without special punctuation) and provide the electronic address in parentheses, as in these samples:

> The Victorian Web presents a wide range of information on the period, ranging from discussions of art to important people, from the history of ideas to the elements of popular culture, from science to philosophy, from technology to social history (http://www.victorianweb.org).

> The UNICEF website provides links to a variety of useful sources that discuss the welfare of children around the world (http://www.unicef.org).

To cite a source—an article, illustration, map, or other element—from a professional website, information database, or scholarly project, include the author (or artist, compiler, or editor) of the individual source, if available; the date; and the title of the source, without special punctuation. The retrieval statement includes the name of the website, database, or project (not italicized), a colon, and the site's URL. However, if a website's name is clear from the URL, it is not required in the retrieval statement.

de Vries, S. (2007, November 18). Close encounters with Alfred
　　Adler. Retrieved from Classical Adlerian Psychology
　　website: http://ourworld.compuserve.com

　　In-text citation　(de Vries, 2007)

Hart, M. (1992). The history and philosophy of Project
　　Gutenberg. Retrieved from http://www.gutenberg.org

　　In-text citation　(Hart, 1992)

8j An Online Transcript of a Lecture or Speech

To cite an online transcript of a lecture or speech, first provide the information required for a lecture or a speech (see 7h). Then include the word *Transcript,* not italicized and in brackets, and the retrieval statement.

King, M. L., Jr. (1964, December 10). [Nobel Peace Prize acceptance speech]. Speech presented at Nobel Prize Ceremony, Oslo, Sweden. [Transcript]. Retrieved from http://nobelprize.org/

> ***In-text citation*** (King, 1964)

Roosevelt, E. (1948, September 28). [Address]. Speech presented at the United Nations Conference, Paris, France. [Transcript]. Retrieved from http://www.americanrhetoric. com/

> ***In-text citation*** (Roosevelt, 1948)

8k An Online Map, Graph, Table, or Chart

To cite an online map, graph, table, or chart, first provide the information required for the kind of visual element (see 7j). Then provide the retrieval statement.

United States Geological Survey. (2010, February 6). Parana River Delta [Satellite image]. In *Earth as Art Series.* Retrieved from the United States Geological Survey website: http://eros.usgs.gov

> ***First in-text citation*** (United States Geological Survey [USGS], 2010)
> ***Subsequent citations*** (USGS, 2010)

This image is part of a series, which is identified after the title.

United States Census Bureau. (2008). School enrollment by poverty status, sex, and age [Table]. Retrieved from the United States Census Bureau website: http://pubdb3.census.gov

> ***First in-text citation*** (United States Census Bureau [USCB], 2008)
> ***Subsequent citations*** (USCB, 2008)

This graph is found on a government website.

81   A CD-ROM Source

To cite a CD-ROM source, include the author or editor, the
release date, and the title, italicized. End the entry with
the following information in parentheses: the publisher or
distributor; the word *CD-ROM,* not italicized; the release
date; and an item number, if applicable.

Centers for Disease Control and Prevention. (2003).
       International classification of diseases (6th ed.). (U.S.
       Government Printing Office, CD-ROM, 2003 release).

> ***First in-text citation***   (Centers for Disease Control and
> Prevention [CDCP], 2003)
> ***Subsequent citations***   (CDCP, 2003)

National Association for Sport and Physical Education. (2008).
       PE metrics: Assessing the standards: Standard 1, elementary.
       (Author, CD-ROM, 2008 release).

> ***First in-text citation***   (National Association for Sport and
> Physical Education [NASPE], 2008)
> ***Subsequent citations***   (NASPE, 2008)

8m   An E-Mail Interview

An interview conducted through e-mail correspondence
is considered personal communication. As such, it is not
included in the reference list. However, it is cited in the text
of the paper by enclosing the phrase *personal communication*
(not italicized) and the date of the e-mail in parentheses.

> Davis (personal communication, March 13, 2010) noted
> that classroom technology is only as good as the people
> who use it.

8n   An Online Video Podcast

To cite an online video podcast, provide the information
required for regularly distributed motion pictures or television broadcast (see 7a and 7c). Then add a retrieval statement
for the online source (website, scholarly project, and so on).

Rich, J. (2010, January 6). Wrong place, wrong time:
       Understanding trauma and violence in the lives of young
       black men [Video podcast]. Retrieved from the National
       Institutes of Health website: http://www.nih.gov

> ***In-text citation***   (Rich, 2010)

Ruiz, M. (Producer). (2008, February 21–25). *Autism: The hidden epidemic* [Video podcast]. New York, NY: National Broadcasting Company. Retrieved from http://www. autismspeaks.org

> ***In-text citation***   (Ruiz, 2008)

8o   An Online Audio Podcast

To cite an audio podcast, provide the information required for regular radio broadcasts, recordings, or speeches (7d to 7e and 7h). Then add a retrieval statement for the online source (website, scholarly project, and so on).

Greenfieldboyce, N. (2010, May 7). Stressful decision? Washing hands could help soothe [Audio podcast]. In *Talk of the nation*. Retrieved http://www.npr.org

> ***In-text citation***   (Greenfieldboyce, 2010)

Kastenbaum, S. (2010, May 6). A family fights back [Audio podcast]. In *CNN Radio Reports*. Retrieved from http://www.cnn.com/services/podcasting

> ***In-text citation***   (Kastenbaum, 2010)

8p   An Online Posting—Blog or Discussion Group

To cite an online posting to a blog or discussion group, provide the author, identified by name or screen name; the date of the posting; the title of the posting, with a description of the message; and a retrieval statement that is appropriate to the kind of source.

Wiley, S. (2010, May 6). Looking for work? Consider the healthcare industry [Blog message]. Retrieved from PBS Blogs: http://www.pbs.org/engage/blogs/programs

> ***In-text citation***   (Wiley, 2010)

Yeal9. (2010, May 7). Re: The birth control pill's 50th anniversary: Science, reason, and women's rights [Discussion group comment]. Retrieved from *Washington Post* discussion group: http://www. washingtonpost.com

> ***In-text citation***   (Yeal9, 2010)

1/2 inch

Labeled running head: all capitals (35–36)

Identifying information: centered (25)

If an author note is required, it appears at the bottom of the title page (26).

Beyond Birth Order:

Recognizing Other Variables

Elissa Allen

Indiana State University

1/2 inch

Centered label with normal capitalization (27)

Unindented ¶: 250 words or fewer (27)

Abstract

Although scholars continue to make a case for birth-order effects in children's development, exclusive reliance on this useful but one-dimensional criterion ignores other variables that affect children's personal, intellectual, and social development. The sex of other siblings, the time between births, the size of the family, the age of the mother, the psychological condition of the children, the absence of a parent, and the birth order of the parents also influence a child's development.

BEYOND BIRTH ORDER   3

The text begins on page 3 (28).

Beyond Birth Order:

Recognizing Other Variables

Sigmund Freud, Queen Elizabeth II, Albert Einstein, William Shakespeare, George Washington, Jacqueline Kennedy, John Milton, Julius Caesar, Leontyne Price, and Winston Churchill. What do these famous people have in common? They were all first-born children. The fact that so many important people in all spheres of influence have been first-born children lends credence to the notion that birth order helps determine the kind of people we become.

Scientific studies over the years have, in fact, suggested that birth order affects an individual's development. For example, Pine (1995) suggested that first-born children acquire language skills sooner than later-born children. Skinner and Fox-Francoeur (2010) observed that first-born children use established procedures to solve problems, whereas later-born children use less predictable strategies. Kluger (2007) noted that later-born children are more inclined toward risky activities than are first-born children, and Sulloway (1995) observed that later-born children are more rebellious than first-born children. Further, Ernst and Angst (1983) explained the underlying premise of birth-order effects this way: "Everybody agrees that birth-order differences must arise from differential socialization by the parents. There is, however, no general theory on how this differential socialization actually works" (p. x). Yet other studies (Herrera, Zajonc, Wieczorkowska, & Cichomski, 2003) suggested that parents' beliefs about birth-order

Centered title with headline-style capitalization (28)

Allusions as an introductory strategy

Historical context established

Past tense to describe scholarship (54)

General reference: author and date (67)

Specific reference: author, date, and page (70)

differences influence their expectations for their children. Stein (2008) also observed that birth-order effects are more pronounced in families that are competitive and democratic. It is not surprising, then, that a general theory has not emerged because many other variables besides birth order influence an individual's personal, intellectual, and social development.

Thesis statement (2–3)

Sex of the Siblings

Headings to divide the discussion (36–37)

While acknowledging that birth order plays a part in an individual's development, scholars have begun to recognize that it is only one variable. For example, Sutton-Smith and Rosenberg (1970) observed that even in two-child families there are four possible variations for sibling relationships based on gender: (a) first-born female, second-born female; (b) first-born female, second-born male; (c) first-born male, second-born male; (c) first-born male, second-born female. In families with three children, the variations increase to 24. To suggest that being the first-born child is the same in all of these contexts ignores too many variables.

Elements in a series (35)

Common knowledge suggests that the number increases to 24 (16–17).

Time Between Births

Summary of Forer's ideas

Forer (1976) suggested that when the births of children are separated by five or more years, the effects of birth order are changed. For example, in a family with four children (with children aged 12, 6, 4, and 2 years old), the second child would be more likely to exhibit the characteristics of an oldest child because of his or her nearness in age to the younger children and the 6-year separation in age from the oldest child. The pattern would differ from that of a

Comparative numbers in the same form (50)

BEYOND BIRTH ORDER   5

sibling in a four-child family if the children were
spaced fewer than three years apart (for example,
if the children were 10, 8, 5, and 3 years old); this
second child would exhibit the characteristics typical
of a second–middle child.

Elissa's own
example: no
documentation
required

Size of Family

Studies have also suggested that the size of the
family modifies the effects of birth order. In a
moderate-sized family (two to four children), the
first-born child usually achieves the highest level of
education; however, Forer (1969) observed that
"a first-born child from a large family has often been
found to obtain less education than a last-born child
from such a family" (p. 24). Whether this occurs
because large families tend to have lower
socioeconomic status or whether it is the result of
varied family dynamics, the overall size of the family
seems to alter the preconceived notions of birth order
and its influence on a child's development
(Hartshorne, 2010).

Last names
only

Age of the Mother

Studies have suggested that a mother's age has a
strong bearing on the child's learned behavior, regard-
less of birth order (Booth & Kee, 2009). Sutton-Smith
and Rosenberg (1970) offered this perspective:

> On a more obvious level, younger mothers have
> more stamina and vigor than older mothers. One
> speculation in the literature is that they are also
> more anxious and uncertain about their child-
> training procedures, and that this has an effect of
> inducing anxiety in their offspring. (p. 138)

Long quota-
tion: 5-space
indentation
(72–73)

Set-in quota-
tion: period
before the
citation (72–73)

BEYOND BIRTH ORDER   6

It seems safe to assume, then, that the third child of a woman of 28 will have a different experience growing up than the third child of a woman of 39. They may share the same relational patterns with their siblings, but they will not share the same patterns with their mothers.

Psychological Factors

Early studies on birth order failed to account for psychological differences among children, even among those who shared the same birth status. Forer (1969) asserted, however, that "special conditions involving a child in a family may change the birth-order effect both for him and his siblings" (p. 19). Such conditions as a child's mental retardation, severe hearing loss, blindness, disabling handicaps—or even extreme beauty, exceptional intelligence, or great physical skill—can alter the dynamics of the family and consequently affect the traditionally described effects of birth order. In short, a middle child whose physiological conditions are outside the normal spectrum—because of different potential and opportunity—will not have the same life experiences as a middle child who is considered average.

Summary of ideas

Absence of a Parent

Parents may be absent from family units for a variety of reasons: A parent may die, creating a permanent void in a family unit; a parent may be gone to war or be hospitalized for an extended period, creating a temporary but still notable disruption in the family; or a parent may travel for business, creating an irregular but obvious interruption in the family's normal workings. The loss of a parent can affect a

BEYOND BIRTH ORDER   7

child's experiences and can, under certain circumstances, mitigate the effects of birth order (Sulloway, 1997). Toman (1993) explained that the effects will be greater

    a. The more recently they have occurred,

    b. The earlier in a person's life they have occurred,

    c. The older the person lost is (in relation to the oldest family member),

    d. The longer the person has lived together with the lost person,

    e. The smaller the family,

    f. The greater the imbalance of the sexes in the family resulting from the loss,

    g. The longer it takes the family to find a replacement for the lost person,

    h. The greater the number of losses, and the graver the losses, that have occurred before. (pp. 41–42)

A long quote (72–73)

Such disruptions—whether major or minor—alter the family unit and often have a greater influence on the children than the traditional effects of birth order.

Birth Order of Parents

A number of scholars have asserted that the birth order of parents influences to a high degree their interrelationships with their children and, consequently, creates an impact that extends beyond the simple birth order of the children. Toman (1993) described the family relationships, based on birth order, that promise the least conflict and, consequently, best situation for children's development:

If the mother is the youngest sister of a brother and has an older son and a younger daughter, she can identify with her daughter and the daughter with the mother. The daughter, too, is the younger sister of a brother. Moreover, the mother has no trouble dealing with her son, for she had an older brother in her original family and her son, too, is an older brother of a sister. (p. 199)

Toman's assumption that parents relate better to their children when they have shared similar sibling-related experiences leads to this assumption: When parents can create a positive and productive home environment (because of familiar familial relationships), the children will benefit. When conflict occurs because sibling relations are unfamiliar, everyone suffers. Parent–child relationships—determined, at least in part, by the parents' own birth orders—would consequently vary from family to family, even when children of those families share the same birth order.

Conclusion

According to U.S. Census information, collected from 92,119 randomly selected mothers, 28% of children are first born, 28% second born, 20% middle born, and 18% youngest born (cited in Simpson, Bloom, Newlon, & Arminio, 1994). As long as census takers, scholars, family members, parents, and children think in terms of birth order, we will have an oversimplified perspective of why children develop as they do. Yet studies (Parish, 1990) have suggested that adolescents recognize that family structure and personal interaction have a stronger bearing on their perceptions of themselves, other family members, and their families than do birth order or even gender. And, importantly, websites such as Matthias Romppel's Birth Order Research (2008) approach the issue

Percentages in numeral-symbol form (50)

Multiple authors: joined by an ampersand (64)

BEYOND BIRTH ORDER　　　　　9

cautiously, suggesting that birth-order effects on children are changeable (http://www.romppel.de/birth-order). Perhaps we should take our cues from these young people and current scholars and recognize that birth order is but one interesting variable in personality development.

A reference to a complete website occurs in the paper but does not appear in the reference list (112).

Sequential
page numbers
(29)

Descriptive
title: centered
(61)

Italicized, not
underlined
(49)

Author names
repeated in
subsequent
citations (66)

A DOI is used
instead of a
full retrieval
statement
(106).

References

Booth, A. L., & Kee, H. J. (2009). Birth order matters: The effect of family size and birth order on educational attainment. *Journal of Population Economics, 22,* 367–397. doi: 10.1007/s00148-007-0181-4

Ernst, C., & Angst, J. (1983). *Birth order: Its influence on personality.* Berlin, Germany: Springer.

Forer, L. K. (1969). *Birth order and life roles.* Springfield, IL: Thomas.

Forer, L. K. (1976). The birth order factor: How your personality is influenced by your place in the family. New York, NY: McKay.

Hartshorne, J. K. (2010). Ruled by birth order? *Scientific American Mind, 20*(7), 18–19.

Herrera, N. C., Zajonc, R. B., Wieczorkowska, G., & Cichomski, B. (2003). Beliefs about birth rank and their reflection in reality. *Journal of Personality and Social Psychology 85*(1), 142–150. doi:10.1037/0022-3514.85.1.142

Kluger, J. (2007, October 29). The power of birth order. *Time, 170*(18), 42–48.

Parish, T. S. (1990). Evaluations of family by youth: Do they vary as a function of family structure, gender, and birth order? *Adolescence, 25,* 353–356.

Pine, J. M. (1995). Variations in vocabulary development as a function of birth order. *Child Development, 66,* 272–281.

Simpson, P. W., Bloom, J. W., Newlon, B. J., & Arminio, L. (1994). Birth-order proportions of the general population in the United States. *Individual Psychology: Journal of Adlerian Theory, 50,* 173–182.

BEYOND BIRTH ORDER   11

Skinner, N. F., & Fox-Francoeur, C. A. (2010).
     Personality implications of adaption–innovation:
     Birth order as a determinant of cognitive style.
     Social Behavior and Personality, 38, 237–240.
     doi: 10.2224/sbp.2010.38.2.237

Stein, H. T. (2008). Adlerian overview of birth order
     characteristics. Retrieved from the Alfred Adler
     Institute of San Francisco website: http://
     ourworld.compuserve.com/homepages/hstein/
     birthord.htm

Sulloway, F. J. (1995). Birth order and evolutionary
     psychology: A meta-analytic overview.
     Psychological Inquiry, 6(1), 75–80.

Sulloway, F, J. (1997). *Born to rebel: Birth order,*
     family dynamics, and creative lives. New York,
     NY: Vintage Books.

Sutton-Smith, B., & Rosenberg, B. G. (1970). *The*
     sibling. New York, NY: Holt.

Toman, W. (1993). *Family constellation: Its effects on*
     personality and social behavior. New York, NY:
     Springer.

First lines at the normal margin; subsequent lines indented (63)

Labeled
running head:
all capitals
(35–36)

Running head: STUDENTS' REACTIONS   1

Identifying
information:
centered (25)

If an author
note is
required, it
appears at the
bottom of the
title page (26).

Students' Reactions to Kinds of Test Questions:

A Piece of the Test-Anxiety Puzzle

Gabriel Stevenson

Indiana State University

STUDENTS' REACTIONS   2

Centered label
with normal
capitalization
(27)

Unindented ¶:
250 words or
fewer (27)

Abstract

The purpose of this brief study was to determine
whether specific kinds of test questions produced
anxiety in students. The results of a survey of 89 high
school freshmen indicate that true/false, multiple-
choice, and matching are low-anxiety question
formats, whereas essay, fill-in-the-blank, and listing
are high-anxiety question formats. However, the study
revealed that students' anxiety levels related to
question types do not vary dramatically, either by
question type or by students' performance levels, as
indicated by previous grades.

STUDENTS' REACTIONS

3   The text begins on page 3 (28).

Students' Reactions to Kinds of Test Questions:
A Piece in the Test-Anxiety Puzzle

Centered title with headline-style capitalization (28)

Today's students are faced with an increasing number of tests. Not only do they take tests for their individual classes, but they also take state-mandated competency tests to progress through school and standardized achievement tests to gain admission to colleges and universities. With the emphasis currently being placed on tests, it is no wonder that many students are now experiencing test anxiety.

Unlabeled introduction: contextualizes the paper, clarifies the topic (28)

One area, however, has not received sufficient attention: students' reactions to specific kinds of test questions. Consequently, using data collected from a sampling of high school students, this brief study attempts to discover with what types of test questions students are most comfortable and what kinds of questioning techniques produce the greatest amount of insecurity or anxiety.

The nature of students' test anxiety has been—and continues to be—studied by scholars in education, psychology, and related fields. By understanding the forms, causes, and results of test anxiety, they hope to provide the means for students and educators to address the problem in helpful ways.

Literature review as part of introduction (28)

Spielberger and Vagg (1995) have discussed testing in a large cultural context, cataloging the ever-increasing number of tests used in educational and work-related settings. Wigfield and Eccles (1989) have described the nature of test anxiety, providing useful categories and explanations to enhance the understanding of this multifaceted problem. Others have contextualized the testing situation by describing

STUDENTS' REACTIONS 4

the high-stakes educational environments in which tests are given (Cizek & Burg, 2006; Hancock, 2001).

Scholars have also explored the cognitive processes that are related to test anxiety. Schutz, Davis, and Schwanenflugel (2002) have distinguished between high and low levels of test anxiety and have discussed the ways students perceive the test-taking process and the ways they cope. Others have addressed students' self-awareness about the emotional nature of the testing process and their own procedures for handling emotion during testing (Weiner, 1994; Zeidner, 1995a, 1995b, 2007). Birenbaum (2007) has extended discussions of test anxiety to incorporate students' instructional preferences and learning strategies.

Yet other scholars have discussed test anxiety among special student populations. Swanson and Howell (1996) have expressed particular concern that test anxiety among students with disabilities can lead to poor test performance, which in turn can lead to poor overall academic performance and low self-esteem. Further, Nelson, Jayanthi, Epstein, and Bursuck (2000) have presented information on alternatives to and adaptations of traditional testing that can allow special-needs students to demonstrate what they know without the additional burden of test anxiety.

These studies have laid a contextual groundwork for further study, which needs to include research in areas such as test design and test preparation. This brief survey-based study may advance this work in a small but important way.

Multiple references, separated by semicolons (69)

STUDENTS' REACTIONS 5

Method

Participants

The survey group was composed of 89 high school freshmen (44 females and 45 males) from three classes. The students were enrolled in a required (and untracked) freshman English class that included students of varied abilities at a consolidated high school in west-central Indiana. The students had completed one grading period; their grades from the previous term ranged from *A* to *F*.

Materials

Students were given a brief questionnaire (see Appendix) that included these elements: (a) an element to determine gender, (b) an element to record their grades in English during the previous 9 weeks, and (c) a six-element questionnaire using a Likert-type scale so that students could indicate their anxiety-related responses to six types of test questions.

Procedures

The students' teacher distributed the questionnaire at the beginning of each of the three class periods and read the instructions aloud, emphasizing that students should respond to the types of questions based on their entire testing experiences, not just those on English tests. Students were then given 10 minutes to complete the questionnaire; most completed the questionnaires in fewer than 5 minutes.

Results

The most general analysis of the data involved computing students' ratings of question types using the Likert-type scale (1–2 = *secure*, 3–4 = *no reaction*, 5–6 = *insecure*). Percentages of students' responses appear in Table 1.

Level-1 headings for major subtopics (36)

"Method" subsection: level-2 headings (36)

In-text reference to an appendix (33)

Description of materials and procedures (29)

"Results" section: summarizes the data (29)

In-text reference to a table (30)

STUDENTS' REACTIONS   6

Low-Anxiety Question Types

The findings indicated that true/false test questions created the least anxiety, with 31.4% of students giving it a 1 rating; in addition, 81.9% rated true/false as a 1, 2, or 3, indicating little anxiety. Matching and multiple-choice questions also achieved low anxiety ratings, with 25.8% of students giving them a 1 rating; 79.7% rated matching as a 1, 2, or 3, indicating little anxiety. Interestingly, 84.3% rated multiple-choice questions as a 1, 2, or 3, making it the question type that produces the least anxiety in the greatest percentage of students.

High-Anxiety Question Types

The findings indicated that essay questions created the most anxiety, with 49.4% of students giving them a 6 rating; further, 71.9% rated essay questions as a 4, 5, or 6, indicating a high degree of anxiety. Fill-in-the-blank questions also achieved a high-anxiety rating, with 24.6% of students giving them a 6 rating; 65.1% rated fill-in-the-blank questions as a 4, 5, or 6, indicating a high degree of anxiety. Finally, 21.4% of students rated listing questions as a 6; 65.3% rated them as a 4, 5, or 6, making this a high-stress question type.

Mean Responses

The mean responses to the question types (1–2 = *secure*, 3–4 = *no reaction*, 5–6 = *insecure*) correlated with the individual low-anxiety and high-anxiety ratings given by students, as shown in Figure 1. True/false (2.35), multiple-choice (2.43), and matching (2.53) remained in the low-anxiety category, but multiple-choice and matching reversed their rating

Subsection: level-2 headings (36)

The summary correlates with tables or figures.

In-text reference to a figure (32)

order. Essay (4.56), fill-in the blank (4.27), and listing (4.16) remained in the high-anxiety category; they retained the same rating order.

As Figure 1 illustrates, mean responses by students' grade categories showed slightly varied preferences among high-performing and low-performing students: *A* students (1: matching; 2: multiple-choice; 3: true/false; 4: fill-in-the-blank; 5–6: listing and essay), *B* students (1: multiple-choice; 2: matching; 3: true/false; 4: listing; 5–6: fill-in-the-blank and essay), *C* students (1: matching; 2: multiple-choice; 3: true/false; 4–5: fill-in-the-blank and listing; 6: essay), *D* students (1: true/false; 2: multiple-choice; 3: matching; 4: listing; 5: fill-in-the-blank; 6: essay), and *F* students (1: true/false; 2: multiple-choice; 3: matching; 4: listing; 5: fill-in-the-blank; 6: essay).

An average of the mean responses to all six question types for each grade category indicated an increasing degree of anxiety: for *A* students, the averaged mean response was 2.75; for *B* students, 3.08; for *C* students, 3.57; for *D* students, 3.61; and for *F* students, 3.83. Although the increments were small, there was a steady progression from one student group to the next; however, none of the averaged means fell far from the 3–4 range (*no reaction*), suggesting that, generally, no question format made students as a group feel either very secure or very anxious.

Discussion

The data indicate that, for students, question types fall into two distinct groups: low-stress questions (true/false, multiple-choice, matching) and high-stress questions (listing, fill-in-the-blank, essay).

"Discussion" section: comments on the data, correlates with the hypothesis (29)

STUDENTS' REACTIONS 8

However, the data also indicate that, on average, students' anxiety levels related to question types do not vary greatly (mean responses ranged from 2.75 for A students to 3.83 for F students), which suggests that although question-related anxiety exists, it is not dramatic.

An analysis of the data further indicates that low-anxiety questions (true/false, multiple-choice, matching) are format based, providing information and allowing students to select among options.

In contrast, high-anxiety questions (listing, fill-in-the-blank, essay) are open-ended, requiring students to recall and arrange information on their own.

A comment on the value of the study (29)

The results of this brief study are, of course, tentative and need to be reproduced with a larger, more comprehensive sample. However, the study does suggest the value of analyzing specific question formats because they can contribute in a small but significant way to overall test anxiety.

STUDENTS' REACTIONS

References

Birenbaum, M. (2007). Assessment and instructional preferences and their relationship with test anxiety and learning strategies. *Higher Education, 53,* 749–768. doi: 10.1007/s10734-005-4843-4

Cizek, J. C., & Burg, S. S. (2006). *Addressing test anxiety in a high-stakes environment.* Thousand Oaks, CA: Corwin Press.

Hancock, D. R. (2001). Effects of test anxiety and evaluative threat on students' achievement and motivation. *The Journal of Educational Research, 94,* 284–290.

Nelson, J. S., Jayanthi, M., Epstein, M. H., & Bursuck, W. D. (2000). Student preferences for adaptations in classroom testing. *Remedial and Special Education, 21*(1), 41–52.

Schutz, P. A., Davis, H. A., & Schwanenflugel, P. J. (2002). Organization of concepts relevant to emotions and their regulation during test taking. *The Journal of Experimental Education, 70*(4), 316–342.

Spielberger, C. D., & Vagg, P. R. (Eds.). (1995). *Test anxiety: Theory, assessment and treatment.* Washington, DC: Taylor.

Swanson, S., & Howell, C. (1996). Test anxiety in adolescents with learning disabilities and behavior disorders. *Exceptional Children, 62,* 389–397.

Weiner, B. (1994). Integrating social and personal theories of achievement striving. *Review of Educational Research, 64,* 557–573.

Reference list: alphabetized, double-spaced (61)

Italicized, not underlined (49)

First lines at the normal margin; subsequent lines indented (63)

STUDENTS' REACTIONS 10

Wigfield, A., & Eccles, J. S. (1989). Test anxiety in elementary and secondary school students. *Educational Psychologist, 24,* 159–183.

Zeidner, M. (1995a). Adaptive coping with test situations: A review of the literature. *Educational Psychologist, 30,* 123–133.

Zeidner, M. (1995b). Coping with examination stress: Resources, strategies, outcomes. *Anxiety, Stress, and Coping, 8,* 279–298.

Zeidner, M. (2007). Test anxiety in educational contexts: Concepts, findings, and future directions. In P. A. Schutz & R. Pekrun (Eds.), *Emotion in education* (pp. 165–184). In *Educational Psychology Series*. Burlington, MA: Academic Press.

Names repeated in subsequent entries (66)

STUDENTS' REACTIONS

11

Sequential page numbers (29)

Numbered table on a separate page (30)

Table title in italics (31)

Ruled lines to separate elements (31)

Column spacing is adjusted for easy reading (31).

Table 1

Overall Responses (Security to Insecurity) to Question Types

Question type	Rating					
	1	2	3	4	5	6
Matching	25.8	30.3	23.6	11.2	3.4	5.6
True/false	31.4	25.8	24.7	13.5	3.4	1.1
Fill-in-the-blank	2.2	10.1	22.5	13.5	27.0	24.6
Multiple-choice	25.8	32.6	25.9	6.7	6.7	2.2
Listing	4.5	5.6	24.7	21.4	22.5	21.4
Essay	6.8	13.5	7.9	10.1	12.4	49.4

STUDENTS' REACTIONS

Numbered figure on a separate page (32)

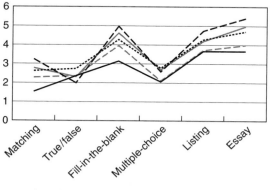

——— A student
– – – B student
·········· C student
——— D student
– – – F student

Figure 1. Mean responses to questions by student grade categories.

STUDENTS' REACTIONS   13

Appendix

Test Anxiety Questionnaire

Survey: Test Anxiety—Reactions to Kinds of Test Questions

M   F

Grade Last 9 Weeks: *A*   *B*   *C*   *D*   *F*

Circle one response for each kind of test question: *1* means that you feel *comfortable/secure* with these kinds of questions (you won't worry about that part of the test); *6* means that you feel *uncomfortable/insecure* with these question types (you will worry about how you do on that part of the test). Consider tests for all classes, not just English.

	Secure		No reaction		Insecure	
1. Matching	1	2	3	4	5	6
2. True/false	1	2	3	4	5	6
3. Fill-in-the-blank	1	2	3	4	5	6
4. Multiple-choice	1	2	3	4	5	6
5. Listing	1	2	3	4	5	6
6. Essay	1	2	3	4	5	6

A | Poster Presentations

As alternatives to traditional documented papers, poster presentations provide opportunities for researchers to share the results of either text-based or experimental research in visually oriented and interactive ways.

Poster presentations developed as a part of professional meetings. Recognizing that traditional, speech-based sessions limited the scope of conferences, organizers searched for ways in which to involve a greater number of researchers in conference activities, as well as to provide opportunities for people to share preliminary findings or to solicit reactions to "work in progress." Because poster presentations are now a common way to share research, teachers have begun to incorporate the format into their classroom activities so that students–researchers can develop skills in presenting their findings in interactive ways.

Poster Presentations—An Overview

Poster presentations emphasize visual elements, supported with printed information, and allow researchers to discuss their work with interested people.

At conferences, presenters are allotted a predetermined amount of space (4-by-4 feet, 4-by-8 feet, or sometimes more) in an exhibit hall and display their posters for review for an allotted amount of time (1 hour or sometimes longer). Presenters stay with their posters, explain their work, answer questions, and solicit reactions. The visual presentation of research findings provides an exciting alternative to traditional speeches (which are often readings of papers), and the interactive format allows for more give-and-take among those who attend conferences.

In classes and seminars, poster presentations allow students to present their research to the entire class, as opposed to just the teacher, and to gather helpful reactions to their work.

Features of Poster Presentations

Whether given at a conference or in a classroom, poster presentations share a variety of features, which may be surprisingly simple or highly elaborate.

- *Display surface.* The simplest "poster" can be prepared on a standard 2-by-3-foot sheet of poster board, mounted for stability. Displayed on an easel for easy viewing, this kind of poster is most commonly presented in the classroom. More elaborate posters are prepared as freestanding displays, may include multiple display panels, and may be quite expensive to prepare. Such complex posters are more commonly presented at conferences.

- *Content.* To ensure that people focus properly on your work, create a clear and interesting title for the poster and provide your name and affiliation. Because posters of all kinds must present content in concise, easily readable form, use headings judiciously. The standard divisions of a research paper—method, results, discussion, and others—provide familiar ways to divide the content of the poster, although other organizational patterns are also acceptable.

- *Visual elements.* Because posters emphasize the visual presentation of research findings, use graphic elements to your advantage. Arrange information for easy interpretation, remembering that readers scan visual documents in the same way they read: from left to right and from top to bottom. When possible, reduce material to bulleted lists for easy scanning. Select simple fonts in sizes that can be read from 3 to 6 feet away. Use tables, charts, graphs, and images to clarify ideas. Employ color, when possible, to create visual interest.

- *Supporting documents.* Provide a one- to two-page supporting document that summarizes the information presented on your poster. Label it clearly with the presentation's title and your identifying information; also include key elements from the poster. Make copies for those attending the conference or for class members.

- *Presentation.* You must facilitate the review of the poster. Without simply reading or summarizing the material for your audience (after all, they can do that), highlight key features and direct their attention to the most salient points. Also, be prepared to answer questions and guide discussion.

Suggestions for Poster Presentations

Because poster presentations provide a unique opportunity to share research findings, a well-planned presentation takes time to prepare and requires unique kinds of effort. Consider these suggestions:

- *Allow yourself sufficient time.* Do not assume that a poster session is easy to prepare. Not only does it require initial research, but it also warrants specialized preparation that may be new to you if you are used to preparing only written documents. Also, because the presentation includes more kinds of elements—visual and speaking components, as well as written content—preparing the poster presentation should not be a rushed effort.

- *Experiment with design elements.* Explore alternative ways to design your poster. Prepare material in several formats (try different fonts and font sizes; use different color combinations; prepare tables *and* figures), and then decide which format creates the best visual effect.

- *Solicit reactions.* Seek responses to your work. Ask for overall reactions but also ask specific questions about presentational elements. If you have prepared alternative versions of your poster, ask which is most effective.

- *Practice your presentation.* Although a well-prepared poster should in some regards "speak for itself," consider the ways in which you can help an audience review your poster. Develop a set of "talking points," a brief list of comments to guide your explanations. When possible, practice your presentation to ensure that your expression is clear and helpful.

- *Anticipate questions.* Think critically and predict questions that your audience might pose; then practice responding to those questions.

Poster presentations provide a unique way to share the results of research. Their conciseness, visual clarity, and interactivity make them an effective means to share the results of your research work.

Students' Reactions to Kinds of Test Questions:
A Piece in the Test-Anxiety Puzzle

Gabriel Stevenson

Indiana State University

Participants:	89 high school freshmen (44 females and 45 males), from three untracked English classes; students had completed one grading period, with grades ranging from *A* to *F*.
Materials:	A brief questionnaire: (a) gender, (b) grades in English, (c) a six-element questionnaire using a Likert-type scale to indicate their anxiety-related responses to six types of test questions, and (d) a section for additional comments about types of test questions.
Procedures:	The students' teacher distributed the questionnaire and read the instructions aloud; students were given 10 minutes to complete the questionnaire.

Overall Responses to Question Types (Security to Insecurity)

	Rating					
	Secure		No reaction		Insecure	
Question Type	1	2	3	4	5	6
Matching	25.8	30.3	23.6	11.2	3.4	5.6
True/false	31.4	25.8	24.7	13.5	3.4	1.1
Fill-in-the-blank	2.2	10.1	22.5	13.5	27.0	24.6
Multiple-choice	25.8	32.6	25.9	6.7	6.7	2.2
Listing	4.5	5.6	24.7	21.4	22.5	21.4
Essay	6.8	13.5	7.9	10.1	12.4	49.4

The data indicate that, for students, question types fall into two distinct groups: low-stress questions (true/false, multiple-choice, matching) and high-stress questions (listing, fill-in-the-blank, essay). Further analysis indicates that low-anxiety questions (true/false, multiple-choice, matching) are format based, providing information and allowing students to select among options. In contrast, high-anxiety questions (listing, fill-in-the-blank, essay) are open-ended, requiring students to recall and arrange information on their own.

Index

Sample Reference-List Entries

An Article in a Journal With Continuous Paging (5a)

Harrison, R. L., & Westwood, M. J. (2009). Preventing vicarious traumatization of mental health therapists: Identifying protective practices. *Psychotherapy: Theory, Research, Practice, Training, 46*, 203–219.

An Article in a Journal With Separate Paging (5b)

McDonald, T. P., Poertner, J., & Jennings, M. A. (2007). Permanency for children in foster care: A competing risks analysis. *The Journal of Social Science Research, 33*(4), 45–56.

An Article in a Monthly Magazine (5d)

McGowen, K. (2009, July/August). Out of the past. *Discover, 30*(6), 30–37.

An Article in a Newspaper (5f)

Pogrebin, R. (2010, April 22). A mother's loss, a daughter's story. *The New York Times,* pp. E1, E9.

A Book by One Author (6a)

Weiner, M. F. (2010). *Power, protest, and the public school: Jewish and African American struggles in New York City.* New Brunswick, NJ: Rutgers University Press.

A Book by Two or More Authors (6b)

Wright, J. P., Tibbetts, S. G., & Daigle, L. E. (2008). *Criminals in the making: Criminality across the life course.* Thousand Oaks, CA: Sage.